BMA

The Ultimate AFP Application Guide

ISBN 978-1-912557-59-2

Published by *RAR Medical Services Limited*
www.oxbridgemedicalsociety.com

This book is neither created nor endorsed by any medical school, university, college, hospital or royal society nor by any other body. The authors and publisher claim no affiliation with any medical school, university, college, hospital or royal society. The information offered in this book is purely advisory and any advice given should be taken within this context. As such, the publishers and authors accept no liability whatsoever for the outcome of any applicant's university applications or for any other loss. Although every precaution has been taken in the preparation of this book, the publisher and author assume no responsibility for errors or omissions of any kind. Neither is any liability assumed for damages resulting from the use of information contained herein. This does not affect your statutory rights.

The Ultimate AFP Application Guide

Dr Charles Earnshaw

Dr Rohan Agarwal

About the Authors

Charles is as an **Academic Clinical Fellow** in Dermatology, and is funded by the National Institute for Health Research. He has a strong interest in medical education, and taught Pathology to dozens of undergraduates whilst a student at Gonville and Caius College, Cambridge. Prior to his current post, he interviewed for, and successfully obtained, a place on the Academic Foundation Programme

Charles has a desire to run his own molecular biology research laboratory. He has published in the fields of oncology and immunology, and is working towards his PhD Fellowship Application. He enjoys mountaineering and photography.

Rohan is **Managing Director** at *UniAdmissions* and is responsible for its technical and commercial arms. He graduated from Gonville and Caius College, Cambridge and is a fully qualified doctor. Over the last five years, he has tutored hundreds of successful Oxbridge and Medical applicants. He has also authored ten books on admissions tests and interviews.

Rohan has taught physiology to undergraduates and interviewed medical school applicants for Cambridge. He has published research on bone physiology and writes education articles for the Independent and Huffington Post. In his spare time, Rohan enjoys playing the piano and table tennis.

Foreword

The Academic Foundation Programme offers the first opportunity for aspiring clinician-scientists to secure some protected academic time. As such, this Programme represents a chance to kick-start your future clinical academic career, building towards an Academic Clinical Fellowship application and potentially from there to a PhD fellowship application.

Few career choices offer the flexibility and potential rewards that a combined clinical and academic career does. You have the opportunity to make a difference to the day-to-day lives of individual people you see in clinic, whilst at the same time the chance to improve treatment for a much greater number of people through the research you perform, or education you provide.

The benefits and desirable nature of this career path therefore makes the application to the Academic Foundation Programme a competitive one – competition ratios currently sit at roughly 3.25 applicants per place. Therefore, gaining knowledge about, and making early planning for, the application can be extremely important and useful for applicants. We hope to provide a concise and informative overview of the application process, including what to expect at interview, and hope that this will remove some of the mystery surrounding the Academic Foundation Programme. We hope to not only improve the application experience of those applying, but also encourage other trainees to apply to the Programme who may not have considered doing so in the first place.

We hope you find the book an enjoyable and useful resource.

Good luck!

Dr Charles Earnshaw & Dr Rohan Agarwal

HOW TO USE THIS BOOK

This book is designed to be a comprehensive guide to the full application process for the Academic Foundation Programme. Therefore, it covers preparation prior to completing the online application, through to a detailed discussion regarding what to expect at the interview. As such, early engagement with this book is likely to prove most successful during your application process.

We would recommend reading through the chapters about the person specification and the online application at least a month prior to completing the application, if not earlier. This allows you to plan your application with plenty of time to spare.

Reading through the chapters regarding the interview a couple of times is always a good idea – once to discover what the interview will be like, and potentially remove some of your fears – and once closer to the interview itself to refresh what the day will be like and what knowledge you need to brush up on. Reading these chapters early is also advisable as you may pick up important tips that you need time to implement effectively – such as realising the importance of mock interviews, which can take time to organise.

This book is not designed to tell you what your application and interview style must be like – instead, it provides information and advice based around previous highly successful applications, and lessons that those applicants learned during their application process. Your application must always remain true to you as an individual, and the book aims to give these tips in a way that complements rather than dictates your application. Used in this way, the book should maximise your chances of success in the application. We hope you enjoy your experience using it.

THE ACADEMIC FOUNDATION PROGRAMME

Most readers of this book will be familiar with the Foundation Programme – the two-year training programme that medical students enter following the completion of medical school. It is designed to provide a good level of general experience across a range of specialties, allowing junior doctors the opportunity to experience them prior to making decisions about which specialty they may want to undertake a career in.

For junior doctors that think they might like to have a career that combines medical research with clinical practice, there is a variation of the Foundation Programme (FP) that allows them to have some protected time in which to carry out research of their choice. This often acts as a taster of what to expect when it comes to a career combining research with clinical work. This variation of the FP is called the Academic Foundation Programme (AFP).

The protected academic time within the AFP can be provided to the trainee in a number of ways: the most common is for one of the three 4 month rotations (usually in the second year) to be blocked off specifically for academic time. Of course, the academic time itself can be research (clinical or lab based), education themed or leadership/management themed. Another common way of this academic time being provided is by the trainee having approximately one day per week to perform academic activities. This arrangement tends to favour certain types of AFP over others (for example, it would not work as well with those wishing to perform a lab-based project).

The AFP has a separate application process when compared to the normal FP, designed to assess the potential of the candidate as a future clinician-scientist. This application includes providing a CV, filling in several 'white-box' questions, and attending an interview. We will discuss next the overall career pathway of a clinician scientist, and then for the remainder of the book cover the application process and interview in some detail, in order to give you the best possible chance at being successful in your application.

ACADEMIC CAREER PATHWAY

Applicants are fortunate to be commencing a clinical-academic career in an era where a defined pathway exists that provides dedicated academic time at each of the clinical training stages. Only a few years ago this did not exist, and aspiring clinician scientists had to make their own way through the system, looking for ways to add fellowships to their existing training and take time out of programme to complete research or educational activities.

A detailed knowledge of this pathway is crucial. It provides prospective AFP applicants with an idea of where they should be aiming: not only for the AFP itself, but once they complete the Programme and are looking for ways to continue combining research with clinical work. Indeed, full understanding of this career pathway is very commonly tested at interview, and is rightfully expected by interviewers. Below we provide a flow-chart illustrating the clinical-academic career path. This was produced an annotated by the authors, but similar resources can be found online (for example, the National Institute for Health Research website) if candidates would like more information.

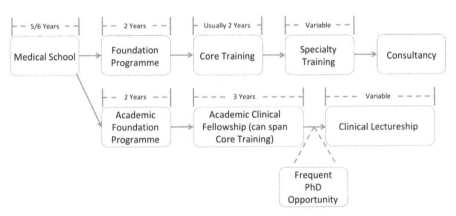

Frequently, clinical researchers will undertake a PhD. There is some flexibility in terms of when one can do a PhD within this clinical-academic career pathway. Commonly, the PhD will be carried out following an Academic Clinical Fellowship. However, there are several other places that trainees can take time out to complete a PhD: some do it in medical school, and others do it after the Foundation programme. There is no one right answer to this, but it is important to give some thought (if you do not currently have a PhD) to if and when you would consider doing one.

THE ELIGIBILITY CRITERIA

The eligibility criteria for AFP are the same as the core Foundation Programme, and are shown below (see http://www.foundationprogramme.nhs.uk for further details).

Applicants must:

1. Have a valid medical degree recognised by the General Medical Council (GMC) by the start of the UK Foundation Programme

2. Expect to obtain provisional registration with a licence to practise with the GMC by the start of the UK Foundation Programme

3. Obtain provisional registration with a licence to practise with the GMC by the start of the UK Foundation Programme

4. Be a UK/EEA national, OR be a final year medical student in the UK OR have the right to work as a doctor in training in the UK, which remains valid until the start of the UK Foundation Programme 2019. Applicants who are unable to submit a valid right to work will only be considered if there are insufficient eligible applicants who have the right to work in the UK

5. Have the written approval of their medical school Dean (or the Dean's nominated representative or the equivalent official to the Dean) to apply for a UK Foundation Programme

6. Be able to start their UK Foundation Programme placement by the relevant start date

7. Be of good standing a fit to practise medicine safely in accordance with the GMC's Good Medical Practice (2013)

8. Have demonstrable skills in listening, reading, writing and speaking in English language that enables effective communication in clinical practise with patients and colleagues as set out in the GMC's Good Medical Practice (2013)

9. Have qualified from medical school within 2 years of the tart of the UK Foundation Programme, OR successfully complete the UK Foundation Programme Office's national clinical assessment

10. Supply all relevant documents as requested

THE PERSON SPECIFICATION

The person specification for the Foundation Programme is shown below (see the UK Foundation website at http://www.foundationprogramme.nhs.uk for further details). It is essential to be familiar with the person specification prior to completing the application – this is especially true for AFP applicants who must complete several 'white-box' style questions, which may themselves directly reference the person specification. You must demonstrate within these questions how you meet each component of the person specification.

1.   **Eligibility**:

- Applicants must meet the requirements as set out in the eligibility criteria (please see the previous chapter)

2.   Qualifications

- Applicants must have achieved, or expect to achieve, a primary medical qualification as recognised by the GMC by the time of the start date of the Foundation Programme.

3.   Clinical Skills & Knowledge

- Be familiar with and able to demonstrate an understanding of the major principles of the GMC's *Good Medical Practice (2013)* (this includes the sections describing: knowledge, skills and performance, safety and quality, communication, partnership and teamwork, and maintaining trust).

4.   Language & Communication Skills

- The applicant must demonstrate skills in listening, reading, writing and speaking in English language that enables effective communication about medical topics with patients and colleagues.

5.   **Attributes**:

- The applicant must demonstrate:

a.   An understanding of the importance of the patient as the central focus of care
b.   The ability to prioritise tasks and information, and take appropriate decisions
c.   An understanding of the importance of working effectively with others
d.   The ability to communicate effectively with both colleagues and patients
e.   Initiative and the ability to deal effectively with pressure and/or challenge
f.   Commitment to learning and continued professional development
g.   Self-awareness and insight into the boundaries of their own abilities
h.   An understanding of the principles of equality and diversity

6.   Probity

- The applicant must demonstrate appropriate professional behaviour i.e. integrity, honesty, confidentiality as set out in the GMC's *Good Medical Practice (2013)*. By the start of the programme, the applicant must demonstrate criminal record and barring clearance at the appropriate level and complete all other pre-employment requirements according to current government legislation.

APPLICATION & SCORING

The application for the AFP is actually almost identical to the application for the core Foundation Programme. This application is carried out through the NHS's online recruitment service, called 'Oriel'. Applications typically open at the start of October. AFP applicants have the option of completing up to two AFP applications after they complete the normal FP application.

The overall process involves the completion of an online application (including the completion of several 'white box' style questions), followed by an interview. The way that the application for the AFP differs to the normal FP is that the AFP application requires applicants to provide information about their prior academic experience and achievements (such as evidence showing publications, posters and prizes), and the aforementioned 'white box' questions.

Following discussion of the application, and for the remainder of the book, we will discuss the interview itself, covering the structure and advice for commonly occurring topics. By applying these principles to your application, you should feel much better prepared for the application, and this in turn should be reflected in your scores.

Application Scoring

AFP application scoring occurs slightly differently than for the standard Foundation Programme application. For the standard programme, applicants are awarded scores for their Academic decile within medical school, based on their prior degrees and publications, and based on their score in the Situational Judgement Test. This then provides applicants with an overall score based on which they are ranked.

For AFP applicants, they are scored based on the decile score along with a score given to them by each of the Deaneries to which they have applied. This score is a result of a variety of factors including the supporting evidence provided in the application, the 'White Box' question answers, and the interview itself. The Situational Judgement Test score is not used directly in scoring AFP applicants, but applicants must achieve a minimum acceptable score in order to be deemed appointable. Applicants with a high enough combined score are then given offers.

THE ONLINE APPLICATION

We turn now to a discussion of the online application process. We cover the different sections of the application, and go into depth discussing the ways your application is ranked. Finally, we provide some suggestions on ways to maximise your application score. It is helpful in this chapter to refer back to the Person Specification to ensure your answers tick all the right boxes.

As mentioned, the AFP application is extremely similar to core FP application. In fact, once the initial FP application is completed, the candidate has the option to submit two AFP applications. You will find that the majority of the information is actually pre-populated based on your answers in the FP application. We will briefly outline all of the stations included in the core FP application, highlighting the significant differences when compared to the AFP programme (as you must be aware of them), before turning to a more detailed discussion of the white-box questions.

Application Sections

The sections for the Foundation Programme (as listed on the UK Foundation Programme Website) include:

1. **Personal**

   - This includes personal information such as your name and contact information, and information about any disabilities you may suffer with.

2. **Eligibility**

   - This section asks you to confirm your immigration status, along with your right to work in the UK and your status regarding pre-registration with the GMC.

3. **Fitness**

   - This section asks if you have any prior criminal convictions.

4. References

- You are asked to provide details of one Academic referee – they must be from your medical school (and they may even be appointed by your medical school to you prior to your application). They will complete an online form as part of your pre-employment checks on your behalf. Ensure you have checked their contact information carefully when completing this part of the application.

5. Competences

- This section requests that you provide details of your primary medical qualification. You must indicate whether you have already gained this, or whether you are a final year medical student (and if so when you expect to gain your qualification).

6. Employment

- This section is left blank.

7. Evidence

- This includes providing evidence of any additional degrees that you have mentioned, or any publications that you have listed. In addition, for the AFP application, there is also space to list up to 10 publications, 10 prizes, and 10 presentations.

- Please note – you must complete this section again in the AFP application, as the information will not be carried over from the core FP application (and the information in the FP is less detailed than the AFP application).

8. Supporting (AFP Applicants Only)

- This includes the crucial White Box questions, which we will discuss in detail in the next section of the book.

9. **Preferences**

- This is the part of the application where you must rank all of the Deaneries within the country in order of your preference. For Academic applicants, this usually aligns with the two Academic Foundation Programmes that you are applying to.

- In addition, for AFP applicants (in the subsequent AFP application) this is where you can rank the available AFP pathways in the Deaneries in which you have applied.

10. **Equality**

- This section asks you to provide a variety of information to ensure applications are treated equally, and includes information such as your age and ethnic origin.

11. **Declarations**

- Finally, there are several declarations that you must agree to prior to submitting your application (such as all the information in your application being factually correct).

Section 8 - 'Supporting'

The main differences when compared to the core FP application are the 'white box' questions that form the supporting information section of the AFP application. These questions, and your answers to them, are important: they are the only chance to really demonstrate your own achievements in your own words, and they are used for both ranking your application and for providing topics of discussion during your interview.

We now list a variety of different questions that can come up, and provide advice for how to answer them most effectively. The word limit for each of these questions can vary between Deanery, and usually is in the region of 200 – 225 words.

Importantly, you can see the exact questions that have come up by looking at the 'Application Supplementary Information' document on the UK Foundation Programme website, which can be found at the following address: http://www.foundationprogramme.nhs.uk/content/academic-training

1. Academic medicine requires an individual to work successfully in a team. Describe a time that will be relevant to your academic foundation training when you have worked as a successful member of a team and identify your role and contribution to this success. Explain the significance of this experience to your application for an Academic Foundation Programme.

This is a very common and important question: the feed rightly suggests that success in Academic Medicine requires the ability to work well within team environments. Here is your opportunity to showcase an example of when you have worked well in a team, and to discuss the relevance of that particular experience to your AFP application.

Common topics for discussion include prior research project experience –potentially clinical or lab-based in nature – as well as teams that were (for example) involved in running a medical student society or other extra-curricular activity. The precise topic isn't necessarily crucial rather than the way you answer the question: you need to discuss your specific role in the team (did you lead it? Were you responsible for organising and coordinating the different elements? Did you have any particularly good ideas that led to a change in the way the team operated, which in turn influenced the desired outcome?), and discuss how you think it prepares you for an Academic Foundation Programme.

This second part of the question is critical. You need to consider what type of clinical-academic career and AFP you would like, and the ways in which teamwork will be important within that. You should then think about the lessons you learned in the experience you described in the question, and about how they can apply to the Academic Foundation Programme.

2. Give two examples of your non-academic achievements and their significance to your application for an Academic Foundation Programme.

This is a question that gives you a good opportunity to highlight how you fulfil various elements within the Person Specification. Discuss sporting achievements, clubs that you have been involved in (and potentially taken leadership and management roles in, such as secretary, treasurer or president), voluntary work you have done (this doesn't have to be medicine related), prizes you may have won in non-medicine related activities and other non-medical qualifications you have gained (for example, musical instruments, scuba diving etc). All of these examples will show that you satisfy different aspects of the Person Specification (that you are capable of 'working effectively with others', have 'initiative and the ability to deal effectively with pressure', are able to 'communicate effectively', and have 'the ability to prioritise tasks').

3. We recognise that applicants will have different experiences in research, medical education or within leadership roles. Please give one example of such an experience or role that you have had in your medical student career and its significance to your application for an Academic Foundation Programme

The example that you provide here should vary based on whether you are applying to an AFP with a research, teaching or management/leadership slant. For example, if you are applying to the AFP with the desire to perform research, then you should discuss a prior research project that you have been involved in. You should discuss your role within the project, what you learned (particularly focusing on the transferrable skills such as teamwork and organisational and time-management skills that will be critical in the AFP), as well as the output from the project (it is always useful to try to slip in achievements in these answers: did the work you did lead to a publication, or did you present at a scientific conference?).

Conveying your enthusiasm for your chosen are is important in this question. This will go a long way to convincing the markers of the question that you are dedicated and truly excited about the AFP, and will show them 'the significance to your application for an AFP'.

4. Describe how you would set out to answer a research question that has arisen from a specific clinical case that you have been involved in.

This is an interesting question, and one that focuses on several principles including Evidence-Based Medicine, and the importance of Literature Reviews. There is no one correct way to answer this question, and it is important that you find your own voice when answering this yourself. You should, however, consider the following approach: make a list of the key questions that have been raised by the clinical question, perform a literature review to assess whether the answer is readily available, and if there is no answer available then consider why this may be and what study might be the most appropriate to address the answer. If you do find the answer, then this can illustrate a good example of Evidence-Based Medicine, and how your practice can be improved by constantly questioning what you are seeing in hospital.

5. Provide a supporting statement about your future career aspirations and why you are suited to your intended career.

This questions tries to assess if you have a clear view of what shape you want your career to take, and if you know how you would like to get there. It also asks you to discuss some personal attributes that you think make you a good candidate for such a career.

You should consider what type of AFP you are applying for, and what type of clinical-academic you wish to be. If you aim to obtain a place on an education AFP, then you should frame your response around this: discussing what you would like your future career to involve (regular medical student teaching? A formal lectureship role?), and the various steps that you wish to accomplish in order to get there (see the Chapter discussing the Clinical-Academic Career Pathways).

The discussion should then turn to why you are suited to this: it is important to be enthusiastic and state that you particularly enjoy, and are good at, teaching, but you need to be more detailed about this. Have you organised and delivered local teaching in your medical student career to date? What other skills do you possess that make you particularly good at teaching (including a discussion of your communication skills, organisational skills and presentation skills).

6. How would training in this AFP contribute to your overall career plans?

You must be familiar with the Clinical-Academic career pathways available – see the earlier chapter on that topic in this book. You should discuss in this question what your aspirations are (is it to be a University-appointed lecturer? Running clinical trials in a specific research area?), and how you think the AFP is the first step in this process. Critically, you should discuss the goals you would have in an AFP (would this be obtaining a PGCE for teaching, or to allow you to develop your research skills leading to an Academic Clinical Fellowship application?).

7. Please describe your experience and achievements as a leader and/or manager.

This can be a difficult question to answer – you are still at a very junior stage in your career after all. Therefore, it is important to realise that this question doesn't have to specifically relate to a clinical topic. You may have carried our a research project in which you had a leadership role, or indeed you may have had a secretarial position in a University Club which improved you managerial skills. You should consider what skills this has provided you with in relation to leadership and management, and importantly how they are applicable to your AFP application.

8. Please describe your previous relevant teaching experience and achievements as a teacher.

In this question you should discuss the different types of teaching experience that you have gained throughout your time in medical school. This may include having a formal role teaching more junior medical students, being involved in OSCE teaching courses, and of course teaching in extra-curricular activities.

You could mention the importance of obtaining feedback from your students, and discuss how you did this (was it verbal or written?) and what changed as a result.

You should ensure you focus also on the second part of the question: a discussion of your achievements as a teacher. Did the medical students you taught do particularly well in their exams? Did you receive good feedback from them? If you were coaching a sporting team did they have success in any particular competitions?

Finally, as we have discussed in earlier questions, it is always important to try to relate these experiences and achievements to your transferrable skillset, and how they have served to further prepare you for a clinical-academic career.

9. What is your single best research achievement and why?

In this question you should try to think of a 'headline' achievement (such as a publication, oral presentation, poster or prize) that has resulted from a prior research project of yours. Provide succinct information about the project, what it showed, what the achievement was, and why you are proud of it. This last point especially will really help to convey your enthusiasm about the AFP, which will really help your answer stand out when the markers are reading the many submissions. You could also then discuss how this achievement and experience further prepares you for the AFP, and more broadly, a combined clinical academic career.

10. Please describe a research project that you would like to undertake.

This is an interesting question: you should do your homework prior to answering this question. You should think about the areas of research that you find most interesting, and that you would like to focus on. In addition, you should look into the specific Deanery that you are applying to, and look for their various strengths and weaknesses when it comes to clinical research. You could look to see if your specific area of interest matches their strengths, and if not if there are ways to link the two.

You should illustrate to the question markers that you are genuinely interested in the research project that you discuss, and should consider the specific ways that you would go about trying to answer your hypothesis.

Conveying your motivation and enthusiasm for answering a previously unknown question is critical here – you should show your question markers that you know how to think of interesting and novel research questions, and that you know that it is important to tackle these questions in institutions that have strengths in similar areas (hence the importance of researching the research strengths of where you are applying in advance).

GENERAL INTERVIEW ADVICE

Before we turn to a detailed discussion of the AFP interview, we will first discuss some general interview advice covering preparing for the interview, how to act in the interview, and how to answer questions. This is going to be the first interview in quite some time for many candidates, and so it never hurts to go over some general tips for success.

How Do I Prepare for the Interview?

You have prepared yourself well for this interview simply by completing medical school and engaging with the Foundation Programme. You already have all of the information that you need. Following the advice presented in this book is useful for preparation – but the most useful preparation you can do is to have a practice interview.

Ask local consultants, registrars and current AFPs in your hospital if they would be willing to organise a brief practise interview for you. You would be surprised at how many of your senior colleagues will go out of their way to organise this one lunch or after work for you. Practice interviews are best with someone you do not know very well - even easy questions may be harder to articulate out loud and on the spot to a stranger.

A practice interview lets you have a go at some of the questions that you will have prepared in advance (see later chapters) and see if they work for you under an interview circumstance. Your interviewers will then be able to give you feedback on these answers, which will be invaluable when tweaking your answers to be the best they can be. In addition, being put under pressure with an unfamiliar clinical scenario will stand you in excellent stead when it comes to that section of the interview. During your practice interview, try to eliminate hesitant words like "Errrr...." and "Ummm..." as these will make you appear less confident. Ask for feedback on the speed, volume, and tone of your voice.

A second extremely useful way of preparing is to attend a locally run AFP interview preparation day if your University offers one. If you don't know if your local deanery has these then ask some AFPs in the above years and the teaching organisers if they know about any days like this. If you still can't find any, then you can also ask friends in neighbouring deaneries if they know preparation days being run where they are. These days are typically run in larger groups than any mock interviews you might organise, but they give another opportunity to practice your interview skills and get feedback on your answers.

Finally, in preparing for the interview, make sure you take sufficient time to review your CV and achievements thoroughly. Make sure you know the details about all of your prior research projects or educational activities: they may well be asked about in the interview, and very little comes across worse to examiners than someone who is unable to basic details about previous experiences.

If you are interested in a performing research-oriented AFP, then ensure you have looked at up-to-date advances in your chosen field, and investigate the research being performed within that field in the deanery you are interviewing at. This will allow you to demonstrate that you are enthusiastic and motivated, that you are a good match to that deanery, and will allow you the opportunity to ask insightful questions later in the interview.

Professionalism and Dress-Code

Remembering that the Consultants holding the interviews are looking for their future colleagues, and indeed the future clinical academic leaders within the NHS, and so it is vital that you maintain a professional approach before, during and after the interview. You should make sure you arrive early at your destination. You should plan the route well in advance, and if you are unsure about the complexities of the journey then it is always wise to make a practice journey prior to the interview.

Make sure you are always polite and courteous to the interviewers. This is an opportunity for the interviewers to assess how you will fit in with their clinical team, and knowing that you are a polite and professional individual with good communication skills goes a long way to reassuring them of this.

Dress in smart attire – you can't go wrong with dress suits. Think about how formal most of the Consultants you have worked with in the past have been. It is important to give off the impression that you are ready to work with them at their level, and therefore dressing the part does make an impact when they are considering the overall suitability of a candidate.

Things to avoid:
➢ Excessively shiny or intricate jewellery
➢ Bold and controversial dress colours, e.g. orange ties
➢ Excessive amounts of makeup
➢ Flashy nails or eyelashes

Things to do:
➢ Carry an extra pair of contact lenses or glasses if appropriate
➢ Turn your phone off completely – you don't want any distractions
➢ Polish your shoes

Body Language

First impressions last; body language contributes to a significant part of this. However, don't make the mistake of obsessing over body language at the expense of the quality answers you give.

Posture

➢ When walking into the room, walk in with your head held high and back straight.

➢ When sitting down, look alert and sit up straight.

➢ Avoid crossing your arms – this can appear to be defensive.

➢ Don't slouch- instead, lean forward slightly to show that you're engaged with the interview.

➢ If there is a table, then ensure you sit around four to six inches away.

❖ Too close and you'll appear like you're invading the interviewers' space

❖ Too far and you'll appear too casual

Eyes

➢ Good eye contact is a sign of confidence and good communication skills.

➢ Look at the interviewer when they are speaking to you and when you are speaking.

➢ If there are multiple interviewers, look at the interviewer who is speaking to you or asked you the question. However, make sure you do look around at the other interviewers to acknowledge them.

Hands

➢ At the start, offer a handshake or accept if offered: make sure you don't have sweaty or cold hands.

➢ A firm handshake is generally preferable to a limp one.

➢ During the interview, keep your hands still unless you are using them to illustrate your point.

➢ Avoid excessive hand movements – your hands should go no higher than your neck.

➢ If you fidget when you're nervous, hold your hands firmly together in your lap to stop this from happening.

How to Communicate Answers

Our objective is not to state exactly how you should answer every interview question you come across. We will provide here some general advice that has proved useful to us – and our students – in interviews thus far, and which will provide a good basis for you when structuring your answers. A good way to ensure you consistently deliver effective answers is to adhere to the principles below:

Keep it Short:

In general, most your responses should be approximately one to two minutes long. They should convey the important information but be focussed on the question and avoid rambling. Remember, you are providing a direct response to the question, not writing an English essay! With practice, you should be able to identify the main issues being asked, plan a structured response, and communicate them succinctly. It's important to practice your answers to common questions, e.g. *'Why do you want to apply for the Academic Foundation Programme?'* so that you can start to get a feel for what is the correct response duration.

An example of this is a question I received at the start of one of my recent interviews. The question was: *'What jobs have you done as part of the Foundation Programme'.* At first I thought this was an opportunity to discuss those I liked, and the main lessons I learned in each job. However, I swiftly realized that this was a question designed to settle me into the interview, and the panel simply wanted to know exactly what they asked: a brief list of the jobs that I had done.

Give Examples:

Generic statements don't carry much weight without evidence to back them up. As a general rule, every statement that you make should be evidenced using examples. Consider the following statements:

Statement 1: *"I have good organisational skills."*
Statement 2: *"I have good organisational skills as evidenced by my ability to continue with my academic work throughout my medical school training. I published a case report last year with one of my consultants, and was able to complete a quality improvement project as well as scoring highly in my exams. I was also able to remain the treasurer of my local football team. The experiences have shown me the importance of good organisational skills in my future career."*

Think Before Answering:

Don't be afraid to take a pause before the start of your answer, particularly if the question is challenging or unexpected. The interviewers appreciate an applicant who takes time to think of an intelligent or thoughtful answer more than an applicant who blurts out the first thing that comes to mind, or one who doesn't answer at all because they become stressed that they can't answer immediately. You should, however, let your interviewers know that this is what you are doing. Say *"I'm going to think about this for a moment"*, or *"that's a good question, I need to think about that for a second before answering"*. Don't take too long: if you are finding the problems difficult, the **interviewers will guide and prompt you** to keep you moving forward. They can only do this if they realise you're stuck!

Answer the Question:

This cannot be stressed enough – there are few things more frustrating than students that ignore the interviewer's questions. Remember, you need to **answer the question; don't answer the topic**. If a question consists of two parts – remember to answer both.

Structuring your Answers

You can approach questions by using a simple framework:

Which **Qualities** can you display?

How can you use your **Experiences**?

What **Knowledge** can you Apply?

How can you give a **Balanced Answer**?

A good when answering questions about personal attributes or skills can be to try and tick off each of these in your answer. This is a good way to ensure that you are not spending too long talking about one thing and so leaving yourself no time to talk about other things. There is little point in reeling off a list of unrelated facts when that would leave no time to show how your experiences apply.

It is better to demonstrate good knowledge and then move on to describe how insights from your prior experiences have also influenced you to give a more well-rounded answer. It's worth practising answering questions using this framework.

The STARR Framework

You may be asked questions where you need to give examples, e.g. *"Tell me about a time when you showed leadership?"*

It's very useful to **prepare examples in advance** for these types of questions, as it's very difficult to generate them on the spot. Try to **prepare at least three examples** that you can use to answer a variety of questions. Generally, more complex examples can be used to demonstrate multiple skills, e.g. communication, leadership, team-working, etc.

In the initial stages, it's helpful to use a framework to structure your answers, e.g. the STARR Framework shown below:

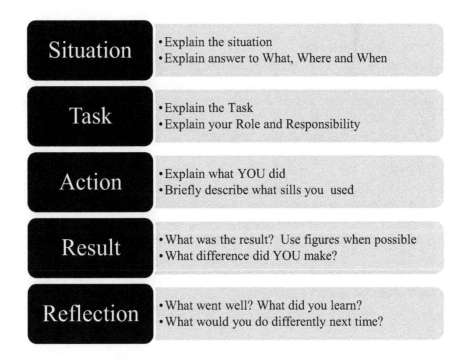

Situation	• Explain the situation • Explain answer to What, Where and When
Task	• Explain the Task • Explain your Role and Responsibility
Action	• Explain what YOU did • Briefly describe what sills you used
Result	• What was the result? Use figures when possible • What difference did YOU make?
Reflection	• What went well? What did you learn? • What would you do differently next time?

We will discuss examples of questions that benefit from using the STARR framework during later chapters.

What Are the Interviewers Looking For?

Many applicants think that the most 'obvious' thing interviewers are looking for is excellent factual knowledge. This simply isn't true. As we discussed, the interviewers want to know if you are someone who can work well as their SHO/Registrar, or as a colleague in the future. As such, they want to know that you possess a number of important personal traits. These include, but are not limited to:

Diligence

Medicine is a very demanding profession and – as you already know! – requires hard work throughout your career. Interviewers are looking not only for your ability to work hard (diligence) but also for an understanding that there will be times where you will have a responsibility to prioritise your medical work over other personal and social concerns (conscientiousness).

Professional Integrity

Medicine is a profession where lives could be at risk if something goes wrong. Being honest and having strong moral principles is critical for doctors. The public trusts the medical profession and this can only be maintained if there is complete honesty between both parties. Interviewers need to see that you are an honest person, can accept your mistakes and are learn from them.

Empathy

Empathy is the ability to recognise and relate to other peoples' emotional needs. It is important that you understand and respond appropriately to patients, relatives and colleagues in a variety of challenging situations. The easiest way to demonstrate this is by recalling situations from your previous experiences as a doctor (one of the many reasons why it's so important). However, it's important to not exaggerate how much an incident has affected you - experienced interviewers will quickly pick up on anything that doesn't sound sincere.

Resilience to Stress

There is no denying the fact that the Foundation Programme is stressful due to the extreme pressure you will be put under at varying times. The interviewers will themselves have been through these stages, and know that the levels of stress can increase as your responsibility increases, and therefore it's important that you have a way of dealing with it in a healthy manner. Interviewers are looking to see if you are able to make logical decisions when put under pressure. Pursuing interests outside of medicine, such as sport, music or drama is often a good way of de-stressing and gives you an opportunity to talk about your extra-curricular interests as well as team-working skills.

Self-Awareness

It's important to be able to recognise your own strengths and weaknesses. In addition, you need to be able to recognise and reflect on your mistakes so that you can learn from them for the future. A person with good self-awareness can work on their weakness to avoid mistakes from happening again. Questions like, "What are your strengths?" or "What is your biggest weakness?" are common and fantastic opportunities to let your maturity and personal insight shine through.

Teamwork and Leadership

Working as a doctor requires working in a multidisciplinary team (MDT) – a group of individuals with a wide variety of skills that work to help patients. The MDT is a cornerstone of how modern healthcare functions. Thus, you need to be able to show that you're a team player. One of the best ways of doing this is by giving examples from your extracurricular activities and from experiences on the wards over the last two years.

Time Management Skills

One of the greatest challenges that clinical academics face is the balancing of their two different jobs. Whilst job descriptions may suggest that a certain job is a 50:50 split between research and clinical work, when you include the extra time needed to write papers, prepare research ethics applications, study for clinical exams and fulfil on call commitments it can feel like doing two full time jobs at once! Therefore, interviewers want to know that candidates can balance the different demands on their time, and they want to push the candidates to find out what coping strategies they have used in the past. Therefore, it is important to prepare for this topic of questioning well.

Academic Potential

Of course, when the interviewers are looking to appoint their Academic Foundation Programme Trainees, they want to know that they have the potential to excel academically. Therefore, expect questions to discuss your previous research experience, previous academic achievements, any prior publications you have and what your career goals and aspirations are.

Interviewer Styles

Although interviewers have wildly different styles, it is helpful to remember that none of them are trying to catch you out. They are there to help you. You may come across an interviewer that is very polite and 'noddy' while others may have a 'poker face'. Do not be put off by their expressions or reactions. Sometimes what you thought was a negative facial response to your reply may just be a twitch. Contrastingly, a very helpful appearing interviewer may lull you into a false sense of security. Rarely, you may get an interviewer who likes playing 'Devil's advocate' and will challenge your every statement. In these cases, it's important not to take things personally and avoid getting worked up.

You don't know what type of interviewer you will get so it's important to practice mock interviews with as many people as possible so that you're prepared for a wider variety of interviewer styles.

Ending the Interview

At the end of the interview, the interviewers may ask you if you have any questions for them. Asking an intelligent question shows that you really care about what you are applying for and where you are applying to do it, and will always come across better than not asking anything. However, don't ask simple filler questions that could be solved by a quick internet search. Your questions should be insightful, and may be about a topic that only consultants familiar with the specific deanery can answer.

You should prepare at least three different questions prior to the interview, in case you are asked at the end of each of the three stations. Example questions include:

"Do your academic trainees have a set teaching programme, and how is the curriculum for this decided upon and delivered?"

"Some of my main research interests are to do with infectious diseases, and I am interested in applying for infectious diseases as a specialty. I wondered if it is possible to use study days to arrange for taster weeks within this speciality? I know that infectious diseases within this deanery is very highly regarded and it would make for an excellent environment to perform registrar training as well as develop my research portfolio."

"I am extremely interested in research, and want to gain more clinical trials research experience. Your deanery has a well-regarded trials centre, and I wondered if it were possible for trainees to arrange some outpatient experience within this department?"

These questions are just examples – the most genuine questions will be those that come from you and are directly related to your interests.

At the end of the interview, look the interviewers in the eye and thank them for their time. You are then free to leave, having completed the Academic Foundation Programme interview.

Final Advice

1) **Don't be put off by what other candidates say** in the waiting room. Focus on yourself – you are all that matters. If you want to be in the zone, then I would recommend taking some headphones and your favourite music.

2) **Don't lose heart** if your interviews appear to have gone poorly. If anything, this can actually be a good sign as it shows that the interviewer pushed you to your limits.

3) **Don't give up.** When you're presented with complex scenarios, go back to the absolute basics and try to work things out using first principles. By doing this and thinking out loud, you allow the interviewer to see your logical train of thought so that they can help you when you become stuck.

4) **Answer the question that has been asked** and try to do so in as succinct and organised a way as you can. This will come across as very impressive to the interviewers if you are able to do this consistently.

5) **Practice.** There is no substitute for hard work. Prepare answers for most of the common questions that come up – see later sections of this book – and arrange as many practice interviews as you can. The myth that you cannot prepare for interviews is just that – a myth!

INTERVIEW STRUCTURE

This is a challenging chapter to write: the different AFP deaneries employ very different interview structures. Some deaneries will choose to have the candidate prepare a presentation and deliver this to the interviewers. Others will provide the candidate with a paper or abstract shortly before the interview and ask them a series of data analysis questions. Most interviews will also include at least one clinical scenario (which can include an ethics and/or professionalism component) and also contain a discussion about your previous research experience and career aspirations.

Of note, it is important not to underestimate the clinical component of the interview. Despite being an interview for an academic post, the interviewers will want to see that the candidate is going to make a competent clinician. This is especially relevant because if they offer you the post, they are essentially removing 4 months of clinical training from your Foundation Programme (and giving you protected academic time in its place). Therefore, putting your best foot forward in the clinical section of the interview is critical, and we discuss some clinical examples later in this chapter to illustrate this.

A common way for deaneries to conduct their AFP interviews is to have a series of two or three stations. The first station might focus on your past research experience and career ambitions, the second may focus on a clinical scenario, and the third may be focused on discussing an abstract or graph that was provided, or giving a presentation that you were asked to prepare in advance. Therefore, when discussing the different sections of the interview that may come up we will treat them as separate stations in separate chapters, though it is import to understand that they can come up in any order and any combination during the interview itself.

In summary:
Usually two to three interview stations, lasting between 10 and 20 minutes each, in one or more of the following categories:
- Academic Station (prior achievements, aspirations and plans)
- Clinical Station (which can include ethics and professionalism)
- Data Analysis Station (critical appraisal of paper, or question about an abstract/graph provided)
- Presentation Station (short presentation prepared by the candidate, usually focusing on the appraisal of a research article)

ACADEMIC STATION

The first station of the interview that we will discuss in detail is one of the most critical: the station where examiners try to find out more about you as an AFP applicant. Expect examiners here to pick up on points raised by you during the white box questions, as well as to focus on your prior academic experience, why you want to apply for the AFP, and your career ambitions. In addition, certain deaneries may also ask you to tell them about a research paper you have read recently: it is important to look at recent issues of journals related to your chosen area of interest and prepare for this question.

This station will last for varying lengths of time depending on your chosen deanery, but expect this to last approximately 10 minutes. As you can see, this is a relatively short amount of time, and so preparing your answers in advance is one of the keys to success.

Sample Questions

We will now turn to a range of sample questions, which are likely to appear in your interview. We will discuss both bad and good responses to each question, analyse why these answers are good or bad respectively, and then provide a discussion of each of the questions. There are different ways of reading through this chapter: I would recommend that you look at the question, and then cover the page and attempt to think or write down how you would answer it. You should then refer back to the text to see how your answer matches the principles illustrated in our examples and advice, and see if there is any way that you can improve on the answer you wrote down.

1) Why do you want to apply for the Academic Foundation Programme?

This is a common question to begin this station with. It represents a good opportunity for you to immediately impress the interviewers with your enthusiasm and commitment to a combined clinical and academic career, and gives you the chance to try steer the direction of the interview by bringing up some topics or achievements that you are particularly proud of and that you would like to come back to later in the interview.

A Bad Response:

I want to do the AFP because I had some really excellent teachers whilst I was at medical school who were truly inspirational, and seeing the difference that made for me it showed me that I would also like to be a teacher. The AFP would allow me to have 4 months to specifically focus on teaching and would also allow me to gain a PGCE, and these opportunities would therefore tell me whether teaching is for me.

Response Analysis:

Clearly, this is a valid reason for wanting to gain a place on the AFP: there are numerous 'education' themed AFP opportunities available each year. The problem with this response is that it suggests that the candidate has very little to no experience of teaching, and so does not suggest that they are coming in with a strong background. Whilst the AFP certainly does help trainees see if education/leadership/research is for them, it is always a better idea to go into the interview suggesting that you are passionate about it based on your prior experience, and to demonstrate how the AFP will further your goals rather than allowing you your first experience of teaching.

A Good Response:

My career aspirations are to be an Acute Medicine consultant and to hold a University Lectureship position. I have participated in several teaching programmes throughout my time in medical school, including a programme I designed and led for the first year students about clinical examination techniques. I loved my time on this programme, and know that I want teaching to play a major part of my future career. I therefore feel that the AFP would allow me to build on my previous experience, and would further prepare me for a combined career in clinical work and medical education.

Response Analysis:

This answer shows that the candidate has a specific career plan and goals, and is determined to achieve them. It shows that they have been thinking about this for quite a while, as they have gained useful experience during their time in medical school to show that they are passionate about medical teaching. It is short and to the point, which is often what interviewers are looking for, particularly at the start of the interview.

Overall:

This is a question that every applicant should anticipate coming up and preparing for: therefore, it gives you the opportunity to briefly explain the type of AFP you are aiming for (education/leadership/research), and allows you to demonstrate that you know what your career goals are and how this programme will help you achieve them. It also allows you to subtly bring up previous achievements (in this case, the programme that the applicant designed for first year medical students), which the interviewers will pick up on and may choose to come back and ask you more about it.

2) Why do you want to train in this specific Deanery?

Do your research about where you are applying beforehand! What are the particular strengths of that deanery? How do they match your career aspirations?

This question can let you score some easy points with the interviewers. It does not take a lot of work – if you don't know already – find out the research or educational strengths of a particular deanery or hospital that you want to work in. By doing this research, you are able to convey to the interviewer that you are taking an active role in your career planning. Personal reasons can be valid, but be cautious about coming across as unprofessional.

A Bad Response:

I really like London as a place to live. It allows me to engage in a wide range of activities that let me balance appropriately my work-life balance. This lets me decompress and relax after work, and so I think this makes me a better doctor. In addition, my long-term friends are applying to train here and so I want to be able to continue to maintain my important friendships with them.

The number of different research and clinical opportunities available in London is incredible, and would let me get experience in a diverse number of different specialties before making the decision as to which medical specialty I want to pursue in my career.

Response Analysis:

This answer does provide a number of good reasons for applying to a specific area. However, this response leads with several personal reasons for the applicant choosing this particular deanery. Whilst personal reasons can be valid in this type of answer, we would advise the applicant do not lead with them. It is important to begin with several professional reasons to show your seriousness as an applicant.

The applicant in this scenario should also probably try to bring up how the London deanery would match with their AFP goals: are they applying for a specific specialty with a specific area of research in mind that the deanery happens to be strong in? Are there good opportunities to develop your post-graduate education skills in this particular deanery?

A Good Response:

My career goal is to be a consultant Neurologist and to perform research in to a number of neurological conditions. I believe this deanery is an excellent place to be a Neurologist as the clinical facilities in this location are second to none. For example, the Royal hospital acts as a quaternary centre for a number of challenging Neurological presentations, and therefore I will have the opportunity to see a number of interesting and rare presentations, which themselves may inform the type of research questions I wish to answer.

During my medical student elective, I was able to spend a short amount of time within the Neurology department at the Royal hospital. I have realised that this is an environment that I would love to work in. In addition, I completed one Quality Improvement project on anti-epileptic drug prescription, and have a second project in the planning stages with two of the consultants in the department. I hope that some of this work could be continued in a potential AFP project.

I have also spoken with some of the academic trainees in years above me, and they felt that the teaching provided within this deanery is very good for AFPs, as there are several specific teaching sessions organised for AFP trainees. This, combined with the world-class research facilities in Neurology, has shown me that this deanery would represent a fantastic training opportunity for me.

Response Analysis:

This is a good answer for a number of reasons. It shows that the candidate has a specific career in mind, and is motivated to achieve this. It shows that they have considered where they would like to do this, and how this particular deanery matches in with both their previous experience and future goals. It demonstrates that the candidate has a relationship with the department and is likely to be successful in getting future projects going. Finally, it shows that the candidate has done their own research to hear about what previous trainees have felt about this deanery, which again shows a strong commitment to this specific area.

Overall:

This question requires a bit of a balance. It is important to show that the reasons for applying to a specific deanery were made because the candidate feels that this particular deanery is in a good position to be able to help them achieve their career goals. A good way is to look at the various clinical and academic strengths of the area, and to see which of these strengths match your ambitions.

The balance comes in discussing personal reasons that have influenced your decision. Whilst these reasons are of course completely valid and make up an important part of your decision, it can come across as an unprofessional decision based on how you phrase it. If it were me, I would just avoid discussing personal reasons in this question. However, it really depends on your individual circumstances. If it is an important reason that will improve your concentration and motivation as a doctor – for example, your children are in local schools – then it would certainly come across as an important and genuine influencer of your decision.

3) What is your biggest achievement on your CV?

Think carefully about your CV prior to the interview. You will likely be asked to submit a CV as part of your AFP application. Therefore, when designing your CV, have this in mind so that things you are most proud of stand out, as these topics can often be used for questioning by interviewers.

A Bad Response:

There are many things in my CV that I am proud of. I am proud of the intercalated degree that I performed, and am proud of the high grades I received at the end of this year. I am proud of the distinction that I gained during my clinical training. I am also proud of the presentation that I gave last year at a regional conference detailing the findings of my Quality Improvement project on venous thromboembolism prophylaxis that I performed as a medical student. Of all of these achievements, I am most proud of my dissertation as this was something I worked extremely hard for.

Response Analysis:

Whilst this technically does answer the question, it essentially comes of as reading a list. It can be a good tactic to briefly highlight several things that that you are proud of that you may not get to mention before focusing on one in particular, but this answer doesn't really come to give a detailed discussion on one of these achievements. The answer also does not show how this achievement makes them a better applicant for the AFP.

A Good Response:

There are several things that I am proud of on my CV, including my First Class intercalated Degree, my QI project, and my strong laboratory experience. What I am most proud of, however, the prize I won at a national medical student conference for my QI project that I performed last year. I investigated the rates of venous thromboembolism prophylaxis that were prescribed in one of my hospital placements. I identified that this was well below target, and came up with several suggestions to improve this, including suggesting there be a box on each admission document that had to be filled in.

This year, I performed a re-audit and showed that the rate of prophylaxis being prescribed has significantly increased. We will await findings to see if this has resulted in a drop in VTE events. I am very proud of this work because I performed the work and suggested several interventions myself, and I feel that I have been able to make a difference in the care of a large number of patients – and that is one of the major reasons that motivated me to study medicine.

This has taught me how to carry out a successful QI project, and the importance that all doctors engage in this activity to improve patient safety. I will look forward to performing further projects during my career.

Response Analysis:

The applicant was able to list 3 impressive achievements, but then quickly zero in on one achievement to avoid the ire of the interviewers. They then explained well what the achievement was, the impact that it has made on both patients and the applicant themselves, and what they have learned going forwards.

Overall:

This is a good opportunity to show of a significant achievement of yours that you may not get to discuss with the interviewers otherwise. Each individual applicant will have a number of different achievements that they can draw on, but the core principles remain the same. Discuss the achievement, what you have learned from it, and how it fits in with your desire to perform an AFP.

4) What is your biggest weakness?

This question often catches candidates out. A careful balance needs to be struck between not coming across as arrogant and demonstrating a dangerous lack of insight (nobody is perfect!). It is also important not to identify a weakness that may make the examiners worry about your safety as a doctor – therefore do not give an answer that can be interpreted as medically negligent. The answer needs to identify a weakness and then demonstrate how you are attempting to rectify this.

Avoid the urge to give an answer that is not really a weakness, e.g. "I'm a perfectionist", as a more profound degree of self-criticism will be appreciated more. Instead, by simply changing the phrasing and customising it to yourself, you can say something very similar, e.g. *"my time management can be a weakness, often because I take on too many projects at the same time"*. You would need to develop this by showing what you've learnt from reflecting on your weakness, e.g. *"...so when I am working on a project, I ensure that I know exactly what the timeline is to completion before taking on more work."*.

Showing humility when answering a question such as this is a good way to make you appeal to the interviewer as a person. Some candidates may be tempted to answer this with a joke, however, this is not advisable as it is a very important question for medics.

A Bad Response:
My biggest weakness is that I'm sometimes quite arrogant. I've always been very successful at most of the things I try and do and so have an awful lot of self-belief. I rarely feel the need to ask for help as I know that I will likely be OK without it. When I fail at something, I get very angry with myself and will often feel down for several days afterwards.

Response Analysis:
This is a dangerous response. Many applicants will indeed be very good at lots of things; however, saying that this has made them arrogant is not good. The candidate states that they rarely seek help for things and have an innate belief that they will be good at anything they turn their hand to. It is not possible to be good at everything from the offset, and knowing when to ask for more senior help is an absolutely critical part of being a doctor. In medicine, it's not just that your ego will be bruised if you fail, but a patient's health may be severely affected.

A Good Response:

I consider myself a natural leader and so my instinct in many situations is quite often to lead the team and exert my authority in coordinating others. However, I appreciate that quite often during my medical career I will not be the most appropriate individual to lead a team. Therefore, I'm working really hard on my skills in working effectively within a team and not necessarily as the leader. In order to improve on this, I've paid significant attention to the feedback that I received during my medical student career from clinical supervisors, looking for specific areas of my team working skills that I can improve. I have also attended a course that illustrated several different types of personality within teams, and how to ensure your personality adapts to the specific team environment. The work I have done has let me become a much more successful member of the medical teams I have been a part in my career to date.

Response Analysis:

This candidate identifies a valid weakness that, if too extreme, would be a problem in medical practice. However, crucially the candidate has demonstrated insight into this problem and how this could be an issue as a doctor. Impressively, they've even shown that they are being pro-active in trying to address this weakness.

Overall:

Medical practice is quite rightly very keen on quality control and ensuring best practice. Therefore, it is essential that those that practise medicine have sufficient insight to identify where they are struggling and when to ask for help. Indeed, many important decisions about patient care are made during multidisciplinary team meetings, and all doctors need to be able to be successful and involved members of these teams. A good doctor will identify their flaws and adjust these so as to prevent the quality of patient care being affected.

5) What are your biggest strengths?

This is a good question to be able to show off what you are proud of within your application, but requires a balance to ensure that you don't come across as arrogant. Consider that the interviewers are looking for their future trainees: they want to know they will be working with successful yet humble applicants.

In addition, when planning this answer, don't forget what job you are applying for. The AFP is a demanding and rewarding programme, and requires good organisational, time management and communication skills. Therefore, consider the elements that are required of a successful AFP doctor, and relate your answers to them. Finally, your answer will always have more impact if you give a specific example illustrating your example.

A Bad Response:

I feel that I make a very good applicant for the AFP because I fulfil the main requirements of an AFP doctor as laid out in the personal specifications: I am hard-working and resilient, and I have good communication skills. In addition, I have good leadership, time management and organisational skills. These strengths make me a good applicant for the AFP, and will stand me in good stead for my combined clinical-academic career post-AFP.

Response Analysis:

This answer superficially covers a lot of the important points for AFP applicants. However, it seems as if the applicant is just reciting the personal specifications. What applicant for any higher medical training programme isn't going to say that they have these skills? Therefore, ensure that you give an overview of your skills, but don't forget to focus on specific samples that make you come across as more personable.

A Good Response:

I believe I have several strengths that would improve my ability to be a successful AFP doctor. Communication is one of the key components of being a good doctor. I have good communication skills, as evidenced by the fact that my communication skills teacher in medical school invited me to be an instructor for younger students.

I also am a very resilient person. I had a very difficult start to one of my placements in medical school as I was in a very demanding ward confounded by understaffing, and came across several clinical situations where I was expected to act as part of the clinical team and felt out of my depth. I was able to remain calm, escalate the situation required, and ensured patient safety was maintained at all times. I was quite stressed outside of work with this, though. I spoke with my supervisor and reflected on these events. I realised that my actions were necessary to maintain patient safety, and this understanding will help me when I am in similar future situations.

Finally, I think that organisation is a key component of being successful in academic medicine, especially when it comes to balancing the ward work, on call rota, portfolio requirements, exams and all that the research component of the job entails. I have been involved in two QI projects and a clinical research project throughout my time in medical school, and have therefore developed my organisational skills in a way that will allow me to succeed within the AFP.

Response Analysis:

This is a good answer for a number of reasons – it discusses several key strengths required of doctors in general, and provides specific examples for each of these. This lets the interviewers gain more of an insight into the applicant's background. In addition, the strengths mentioned focus in on the requirements for success in the AFP, which in turn informs the interviewers that the applicant has given extensive thought into how these requirements match their strengths.

Overall:

Remember, the interviewers are looking at the applicants as potential trainees and colleagues of theirs, and so they want to know more about you and how your past experiences have led you to developing the strengths that you discuss. Therefore, providing context for the examples you mention can be a very powerful tool in demonstrating your suitability for the AFP.

6) When have you had to show good leadership skills?

Being an effective leader is important in a wide range of medical situations: from the acute decisions regarding patient care during a cardiac arrest, all the way to the high-level managerial decisions that many hospital consultants get involved with. A good leader has exceptional communications skills, listens to each member of the team, and is able to make appropriate decisions when required. They must also take ownership of the decisions they make, both during good and bad outcomes.

A Bad Response:
I am at a very junior stage of my career and so it is difficult to think of many circumstances when I have shown leadership skills. However, I did act as the student representative for year in medical school, and so obtained good leadership skills as a result of my role. I attended and organised several meetings during my time in this role, and improved my organisational skills.

Response Analysis:
It is true that AFP applicants are at a junior stage of their career, but it is important to remember the many different opportunities for leadership that you will have already participated in within medical school. This experience may include leadership roles in various clubs within university, teaching positions held, roles taken during volunteering/the elective, and a huge number of other opportunities besides. Therefore, you must have an answer planned that illustrates a leadership experience example, and should be able to discuss your role, what you learned, and how this prepares you to be a future leader within medicine.

A Good Response:
Leadership skills are an essential part of being a good doctor. They allow good communication within a team, and are essential when trying to ensure that a team is running to the fullest of its potential. I took on a leadership role within our local medical student representative team. After discussing the work we needed to accomplish with the other team members, I delegated tasks according to individual team members' strengths, and made decisions regarding where our priorities for our ambitions had to lie. The work that we put in allowed us to change the teaching schedule for the medical students, which allowed for many fewer cancellations of teaching as well as increased opportunity for experiences on the wards. Throughout this experience, I learned the important requirements of being a leader: good communication skills within the team, the ability to make decisions when required and take responsibility for their outcomes, and the requirement for hard work such that I could lead by example.

Response Analysis:

This answer shows much more insight into the requirements of a good leader in the medical profession, and why leadership skills are important. It gives a clear example of a time when the candidate demonstrated leadership skills, the changes they were able to bring about, and the lessons they learned from this experience.

Overall:

This is another question that is very likely to come up, and unless you have prepared in advance, can be difficult to come up with a good example on the spot. The key requirements are to illustrate a good example of a time you have demonstrated leadership skills, what those skills were, and the outcomes of your experience. If you can relate what you learned to your potential future role – as clinical-academics and consultants within the NHS – then that will impress the interviewers, showing that you know what will be expected of you in the years beyond the AFP.

7) Why are good management skills required in medicine?

Medicine is an incredible personal profession –you will be interacting with other doctors, nurses and other members of the multidisciplinary team, and, of course, with the patients and their relatives. Management within medicine can take numerous different guises – whether this is managing a team of doctors, managing a ward, being responsible for coordinating a rota, organising a clinical trial, or making decisions regarding funding. Clearly, the interviewers are not expecting you to have performed any of these roles at this stage – and that is why most managerial courses are aimed at registrars and consultants – but demonstrating that you know about management in medicine is another useful bit of evidence for the interviewers that you are engaged actively in career planning.

A Bad Response:
Medical management is about managing people successfully. This will be important during my future career as a clinical academic as I will be in charge of the medical running of my particular ward as well as my research programme. I will need to ensure that the juniors beneath me have an appropriate level of supervision, that their work-load is appropriate, and that they are happy with their job. I will also be responsible for investigating how to improve the quality of care we provide on my ward through audit and quality improvement. Management will be important to ensure I can delegate enough tasks to allow me to have enough time for my research. I plan to develop these skills during my time in the AFP, and hope that they will prepare me well for my future career.

Response Analysis:
This answer covers some good points – it makes important points about staff morale, quality improvement, and the running of a ward, and touches on the idea of the challenges of doing both clinical work and research. However, medical management experience covers many more aspects than just this, and it would be useful to have discussed some previous experience that can illustrate how the candidate may already have some managerial experience.

A Good Response:
Medical management is one of the core pillars of senior doctors' jobs: both academics and purely clinical consultants alike. They may be responsible for the team of doctors under them, be involved in designing and carrying out quality improvement projects to ensure their clinical standards are maintained and improved, and may also be involved in making important decisions regarding the allocation of clinical funding.

I was elected treasurer of my football club during my time in University. This proved to be a fun and useful role for me – not least because I learned some useful techniques for the distribution of our limited funds in our team. I listened to the other club members, and made decisions regarding the funds allocated to renovating our facilities and to providing out kit. The experiences gained here will serve me useful in the future as I take up more of a managerial role within my profession, especially when it comes to making decisions about where to allocate a limited budget. I also plan to engage actively with learning about medical management. I hope to take some online courses and also to attend taught courses to ensure my managerial skills continue to improve.

Response Analysis:

This answer covers many of the important basics when it comes to the role of management in medicine. It gives an excellent example of some prior managerial experience, and how this relates to the future managerial roles that doctors can take within the NHS. The candidate also demonstrates that they realise that there will be further opportunities for developing these skills and that they intend to make the most of this, again emphasising the commitment to specialty and willingness to plan for a successful future as a consultant physician.

Overall:

Questions about medical management often appear in medical interviews, and will come up increasingly as your experience level increases. At the stage of the AFP interviews, the interviewers are looking to see that the candidates are aware of the different areas that management skills are important in, and that the candidates know how their training will allow them to develop these skills. If you can communicate this, with any specific managerial examples as an added bonus, then you will come across very well in the interview.

8) Can you tell us about a time when you showed good team-working skills?

One of the most important professional skills required in medicine is the ability to work successfully as a member of a team. Team-working skills relate to the ability to maximise the performance of a team of people as a member of the team: this may lead to the improvement of patient safety, the successful running of clinical research or an educational programme, or some other specified team output.

A Bad Response:

During one of my GP rotations in medical school I worked as part of a team of other medical students. We were tasked with performing an audit of patients at the surgery taking allopurinol for gout. We were able to successfully divide tasks between us to spread the work load, and I was always willing to help the other members of the team when they had too much work. We completed the project within the time allotted, and we presented the findings to the rest of the GP team, who seemed impressed with it.

Response Analysis:

This response does not cover any specific skills that fall under the 'team-working' umbrella. These include, but are not limited to, communication skills, time management skills, organisational skills and leadership skills (though being careful not to overstate this component when discussing your role as a specific team member). Therefore, a good answer should give an example – like the answer above – but should explain how your role within the team illustrates these specific professional skills.

A Good Response:

Working well within a team is an essential skill to possess as a doctor, especially when you consider that we will almost always work in teams, and those teams are constantly changing (such as when we rotate jobs, or are on call). Therefore, possessing good team-working skills lets me adapt to the different teams that I work with.

One of the most successful teams I worked with was my high-schools Science team – our team won our regional finals and advanced to the national finals. I was able to communicate well with the other members of the team, ensuring everyone had the ability to give their ideas to the group, and I coordinated different members of the team when we had multiple tasks to perform simultaneously. I provided important organisational skills, providing the documentation during the experimental tasks, which allowed our experiments to be more reproducible than other teams. I also provided good time management skills, which allowed our team to be one of the few teams to perform all of the tasks within the provided time.

During my first ward-based placement in medical school I saw how useful these transferrable skills were – I helped to prioritise ward jobs efficiently, and helped ensure they were completed in a timely manner. I was able to communicate well with different members of the MDT, and successfully contributed to the team as well as someone at my stage of training could.

Response Analysis:

This is a thorough answer that covers the fundamentals of what working in a team means, and what the specific skills required of team working are. Applicants shouldn't feel afraid to give examples that are not directly related to their career to date in medical school. In fact, doing so illustrates to the interviewer that you as a candidate know the importance of the transferrable skills that you gained as a member of a different team as you know the core principles of what are required for a team to work together successfully.

Overall:

Team-working questions are one of the main categories of question to come up during any medical interview. This is hardly surprising when you consider the fundamental role that team-working plays throughout the entirety of medicine. To ensure you are successful with this, you should familiarise yourself with the core principles of teamwork, and to think examples where you can directly relate these principles to your experiences to date.

9) Name some of the difficulties involved in leading a team, how did you make a difference?

Medicine is a profession where you will almost always be working as part of a team. This question is looking for examples in the past when you have worked as a team, but more importantly, the challenges that the team experienced and what you did about those challenges. It is perfectly fine that you had problems working with a team in the past, but the interviewer really wants to see your response to these challenges. This does not have to be related to a medical team (although this can only help the answer) but should show skills desirable in a doctor.

Being a good doctor means more than simply being a good clinician. The interviewer knows that you are capable of leading, but wants you to prove it to them. The way to answer this question is to provide them with a strong example of when you led a team successfully.

A Bad Response:

I do not often lead teams so this question is a little difficult for me. I think I tend to follow the team leader more often, but if no progress is made then I do step up. For example, we were involved in a group presentation and the 'leader' wasn't really leading, so I had a discussion with the other members and it was decided that I should become the leader for this presentation. I was quite uncomfortable with the whole situation but I didn't really have a choice. We managed to get the presentation together after I became the team leader. In this way, I think I did do a good job of leading the team.

Response Analysis:

This answer lacks confidence and assertiveness. These are skills that good leaders should demonstrate when leading their teams. The candidate perhaps did not use the best example of leading from the front as they had not volunteered to be the leader but were coerced into the position. The answer could have been improved by expanding further on how the candidate thinks they did as a leader; did they motivate their peers after morale was low, did they assigns tasks to people?

A Good Response:

I have developed my teamwork skills over my years at school but this has not been without challenges. I really love tic-tac-toe so I quickly joined my school club in Year 9; however, I was disappointed that the club was not running enough events so I met with the president to discuss my concerns and she offered me a position on the executive committee. When working on the committee to organise an interschool tic-tac-toe competition, I had trouble dealing with the treasurer who was not responding to my emails. I arranged a meeting with him and found out that he was having family problems. I offered to help him with his current situation and further suggested that he talk to our college counsellor. I had to delay some of the payments for the event but it all got sorted after one week. I found that by talking to unresponsive members of the team, the real issue could be understood and this helped to build team unity.

Response Analysis:

This response is significantly better than the first, although, note the similarities in much of the content. The first main difference is the person concentrates on what they did within a team rather than talking about how they led a team. The person also brings in a specific challenge that they faced in this team as well as a suitable way of dealing with the challenge (they also showed empathy in this response).

Overall:

This question may throw a few people because it involves talking about a weakness or challenge, but do not be fooled. You should show your strengths by showing how you dealt with a particular challenge. This will be a common theme in questions that ask about challenges that you faced in the past. The main part of this question lies with how you worked within a team to create a positive impact; any challenges that you faced and how you dealt with them also increase the maturity of the response.

10) Where do you want to be in five years time?

This is another question that is important to prepare in advance. As mentioned earlier in this book, a thorough knowledge of the clinical-academic career pathway is critical when it comes to questions like this. You must know how the AFP fits into the pathway, and what the subsequent options for combining research or education with clinical training are. You should have some longer-term career goals that you can discuss in your response. Prior to the interview, I would prepare answers for the '5 year', '10 year', and '15 year' time-frames.

A Bad Response:

I have yet to confirm exactly what specialty I intend to pursue in my future career, though at this early stage I am leaning towards Respiratory medicine, and this is also where my research interests in lung cancer lie. Therefore, in 5 years I hope to be a specialty trainee in respiratory medicine. I also think that I would like to move back to my home in Newcastle so I think I will apply there for specialty training.

Response Analysis:

This answer shows that the candidate has given some thought as to their career goals, but they need to be careful as of course lung cancer as a disease is treated by multiple specialties, not limited to respiratory physicians but also including oncologists (both medical and clinical) and surgeons. In addition, they may be right that they wish to be a registrar in 5 years as this makes sense within the career progression, but they don't discuss how they see themselves fitting into the academic career path – for example, there is no discussion of Academic Clinical Fellowships. The response also doesn't come across as overly enthusiastic, which is critical in this type of question.

Finally, whilst mentioning personal reasons for making certain choices isn't necessarily a 'mustn't do', I would suggest avoiding discussing them unless they are critical for your argument or career choice (for example, the location of your children).

A Good Response:

In 5 years time I plan to have completed my AFP, which I hope will put me in a good position to successfully gain a position as a Respiratory Academic Clinical Fellow. I hope to be nearing completion of my Internal Medicine training, and progressing towards specialty training within Respiratory Medicine. I will aim to continue my research throughout the ACF, and be building towards a PHD application. I am fascinated by the disease of lung cancer, and the importance of primary prevention, and so my research may revolve around that as a potential topic. I also plan to gain my full MRCP qualification during this time.

Response Analysis:

This answer shows a clear idea of what the candidate wants to do for a future career. It shows that the candidate knows the clinical-academic career pathway well, and knows how they want to progress through it. It shows they are aware of various requirements (including professional exams) for their career progression. It confirms that the candidate is thinking about other professional aspirations at this early stage, including higher degrees, which confirms to the interviewers that the candidate is actively engaged in their career planning.

Overall:

The interviewers want to know that the trainees that they appoint to the programme are motivated individuals who have taken the time to think about what career they want to have in future. This is not a difficult task to accomplish – it just requires you spend some time thinking about what topics interest you, and why you think the AFP fits into your larger career ambitions. If you can communicate this to the interviewers then they will have no choice but to be impressed with your answer.

11) Being a successful clinical-academic requires excellent time management skills. Tell me about your time-management skills?

This is one of the most common topics of discussion in these interviews. One of the biggest challenges of being a successful clinical-academic is the balancing of clinical commitments with academic commitments. You will need to achieve the same clinical standards as other trainees at your level, and you also need to continue with your research or educational work to a high standard. Therefore, it can occasionally feel as if you are trying to do two jobs at once! The key, therefore, is excellent time management and organisational skills.

A Bad Response:

During my time in medical school I was extremely busy in the run up to my exams in my 4th year: I had the exams to revise for, I had several coursework submissions due in at a similar time, and I was also competing in my University Squash team in a regional championships. The key for me was ensuring that my time management skills were up to requirements, and thankfully they were as we did very well in the championships and I performed well in the exams. This shows I have what it takes to manage my time well as a clinical-academic.

Response Analysis:

Whilst at first glance this response doesn't seem particularly bad, the examples given are actually quite standard when compared to the things that most – if not all – medical students go through. This isn't necessarily a bad thing, but you need to be explicit with examples that actually show how or why your time management skills are so good. This is lacking from this answer.

A Good Response:

My fourth year in medical school was very busy: I was revising for important exams, I was working in a lab performing research and writing up my project during one of my student selected components, and I was also serving as the treasurer in my University's football team. As a result, in order to continue to achieve at the high standard I aim for, I had to ensure I was organised and managed my time most effectively. I wrote a timetable to work out when I could fit in my exam revision around my lab work. I was able to suggest we move the time of our football board meeting to Saturday morning's, which freed up further time during the week. I was also able to arrange revision sessions with a friend during some evenings in the week, which turned previously unused time into valuable revision time. Therefore, as a result of my proactive organisational and time management skills, I was able to achieve a First Class result in both my exams and my project report, and continued to efficiently serve as treasurer of the football team during this time. The skills I picked up during this, along with the clinical knowledge and research experience gained, have greatly prepared me for the challenges that I will face as a clinical-academic.

Response Analysis:

This is a strong response for several reasons. It gives similar examples to the answer above, but this time provides some more background, which helps the interviewers understand the challenges that were faced at this particular time. It discusses in more detail the various tactics that the applicant used to overcome the challenges that they faced, and then goes on to mention how successful these tactics were. Finally, the candidate mentions how the skills they have picked up will help them in their future career.

Overall:

Don't worry about not being able to think of specific times when you are unsure if you have shown a very high level of organisational skills: the fact that you have made it this far in medical school means that you have many of the skills required. You need to drill down to what those skills actually are, and how you have brought them into use practically, and then need to communicate that with examples to the interviewers. Providing some context of how this fits into your career goals will ensure that this answer is a very strong one.

12) Tell us about a Quality Improvement project that you have been involved with, describing the aims of the project and whether you were successful in making the desired improvement.

It is highly likely that all candidates will have carried out at least one audit or quality improvement project during their time in medical school. Therefore, this answer should be relatively straightforward, but there are ways to score extra points with your answer that you should include.

In recent years, Quality Improvement projects have replaced 'Audits' in terms of the main mechanism by which the NHS wishes to induce positive change in practice. The general principles of QI projects are relatively similar to Audits, but have a more intentional focus on specifically improving quality, instead of necessarily just measuring certain factors or outcomes.

QI projects aim to improve healthcare. As defined by the US institute of medicine (www.ahrq.gov/professionals/quality-patient-safety), improving healthcare in general can fall into the following categories:

1. Safety – that the care we provide is always safe
2. Efficacy – the care we provide is effective in improving the lives of our patients
3. Patient-centeredness – the patient is always at the core of the services we provide
4. Timeliness – ensuring the care is delivered on time
5. Efficiency – ensuring efficient processes exist
6. Equitable – consistency for all patients

Therefore, when thinking about a QI project, it should aim to make an improvement in at least one of these aspects, though of course there is significant overlap between them.

SMART (Specific, Measurable, Achievable, Relevant and Time-Bound) aims are the consensus aims in modern QI methodology that show that the investigators have designed a project that is likely to be completed and to come out with results. An example would be: *We aim to reduce the incidence of hospital acquired venous thromboembolism by 90% by August 2019.*

The different stages that are present within QI projects are described below, and form a circle. This model is described as the PDSA model – Planning, Doing, Studying, Acting, and finally returning to planning again.

1. Planning – this is the process by which a project is considered, and the aims of the project are designed. This may mean looking at a specific process that could be made to happen in a more timely manner, for example
2. Doing – this is actually carrying out the suggested changes
3. Studying – this determines whether the desired outcome has been achieved
4. Acting – this then implements the changes

The PDSA (planning, doing, studying, acting and returning to planning) cyclical model is the approach that should underpin each of the changes implemented in the QI project. It is inherently reflective in nature: so in the above example, if we were assessing the incidence of venous thromboembolism each month, then we would perform a PDSA cycle at the end of each month to determine the areas that need to be improved on in the subsequent month.

If you can demonstrate that your QI project was designed to fulfil these criteria, and that you used a PDSA model to assess the impact that you made, then the interviewers will clearly realise that you have a good grasp of the fundamentals of QI, and that you know what is required to run a successful project.

The Audit Cycle

An audit is a systematic investigation into a system to see how it is performing when compared to national guidelines. It allows us to identify any potential problems that might be preventing good medical practice. Once these problems are identified, changes are made to try to resolve them. After a period of time, the audit is repeated again – completing the audit cycle. Hopefully, the changes result in an improvement in healthcare.

Doctors are encouraged to do audits as they can lead to valuable improvements in clinical care. Audits can occur at many levels:

➢ Nationally, e.g. National Stroke Audit
➢ Hospital-Based, e.g. ensuring that all patients are reviewed by a consultant daily
➢ On a ward, e.g. ensuring that all thermometers are correctly calibrated

A Bad Response:

I was involved with a QI project on an acute medical attachment last year that aimed to improve the number of patients having appropriate blood cultures taken during a temperature spike. I discovered that on a number of occasions blood cultures were not being performed in patients who had a spike in their temperature for a number of reasons, including confusion over what the threshold for taking cultures was, and issues surrounding who was 'qualified' to take cultures in our Trust.

I designed posters showing exactly what the threshold for the cultures were, and what amount of time from the previous spike meant that the cultures would have to be retaken. I also helped to design teaching at the hospital-wide teaching sessions for F1/F2s and CMTs. Finally, I discussed with the medical education department about arranging further sessions for ANTT training. These interventions made a significant improvement in the number of patients correctly having blood cultures performed.

Response Analysis:

This, overall, is a reasonable response. However, it does not suggest to the examiner that the candidate knows what quality improvement specifically means, or the fact that it is different to Audit. Additionally, there are a few things that could be changed to improve it further, such as adding some specifics regarding the success of the project, and perhaps some reflection on what the applicant learned for future practise.

A Good Response:

QI projects are becoming the method of choice when it comes to improving the services delivered by the NHS, replacing clinical Audit. Involvement in QI projects is essential for all clinicians as it allows them to reflect on the quality of their care, and to identify ways that it can be improved.

Using the PDSA design model, I was involved with a QI project on the acute medicine wards in my fourth year of medical school that aimed to improve the number of patients receiving appropriate blood cultures during a temperature spike. I discovered that in 70% of occasions blood cultures were not being performed in patients who had a spike in their temperature for a number of reasons, including confusion over what the threshold for taking cultures was, and issues surrounding who was 'qualified' to take cultures in our Trust.

I designed posters showing exactly what the thresholds for the cultures were, and what amount of time from the previous spike meant that the cultures would have to be retaken. I also helped design teaching to be given at the hospital-wide teaching sessions for F1/F2s. Finally, I discussed with the medical education department about arranging further sessions for ANTT training. These interventions made a significant improvement in the number of patients correctly having blood cultures performed, such that the number is now 85%. This showed me the significant difference that can be made through QI projects.

Response Analysis:

This answer covers the suggestions mentioned above – it gives a clear idea that the applicant understands what QI projects are, and how they performed. It gives a good specific example of a QI project, and clearly states the outcomes of the project. In addition, they state what they learned from this project.

Overall:

QI projects are becoming much more popular with the curriculum organisers the Foundation Programme (and indeed training programmes following the FP). Therefore, a little studying – as described above – will be able to show to the interviewer that you understand that there has been a shift in culture towards QI projects, and that you have a strong grasp of what a QI project is and how it differs from clinical audit. Combining this knowledge with a good example of a project will see you do very well in this question.

13) Tell me about your interests outside of medicine

Having a good work-life balance is crucial to reduce the risk of burnout with the profession: and even moreso when faced with the challenges of combining both clinical work with academia. This isn't a question that asks you to list everything that you like to do outside of work. You can feel free to list a few things, but should then focus on one or two. Ideally the examples should show something about what makes you 'you' as an individual. Clearly, these examples must be truthful, and it would be easy for interviewers to see if this was not the case.

It almost goes without saying, but ensure you do not list activities that can be thought of as unprofessional!

A Bad Response:

I have many hobbies outside of medicine. I like to ski, and have been skiing in the Alps several times in the past few years. I enjoy football, and play in a weekly five-aside game. I also serve as the treasurer of this group. These activities allow me to keep fit. I like to read, which I find this a good way to relax. I also enjoy going to the movies with friends, as we all enjoy reviewing new movie releases.

Response Analysis:

Whilst this indicates a well-rounded person who engages in a variety of different activities, it doesn't necessarily suggest that the candidate is particularly enthusiastic (although I am sure they are) about any of these activities. Focusing more on one or two of the activities can demonstrate the sort of motivation and enthusiasm that translates well into an Academic Foundation Programme trainee.

A Good Response:

I think maintaining a good work-life balance is crucial, particularly as I will be faced with a number of organisational challenges related to combining my clinical work with my research goals, and so I try to lead an active lifestyle that lets me recharge on my days off. I enjoy reading, photography, and working on my website that showcases my photography. However, two of my main interests are skiing and playing football on my local team.

I love skiing, and try to ensure that I go skiing at least once per year. I used to be quite a successful skier, and as a child won several medals in races. I like to read about new technology in skiing, and so I keep up to date with adaptations that I can make to my boots and skis, such as new bindings.

I am also a member of my local five-aside football team. In fact, I am the treasurer for this team, and so as well as keeping fit and providing me with a close group of friends, this provides an opportunity to improve my organisational and management skills. We placed as runners up in a regional tournament last year, and we are working towards opening new training facilities, which will hopefully let us improve even more this year.

Response Analysis:

This is a good answer for a few reasons. It identifies to the interviewers that the candidate understands why having a life outside of medicine is important. It shows that the candidate has a broad range of interests, but zeroes in on a couple of specific interests of theirs. The candidate is even able to discuss the ways that these activities improve their professional skill set.

Overall:

This question allows the candidate to demonstrate real enthusiasm for some genuine interests of theirs. It is very important that this enthusiasm is communicated to the interviewers, as they want to gain a full idea of who you are as a person. Bonus points are certainly available if you can subtly point out how some of your interests improve your transferrable professional skills, such as management experience in the example above. The interviewers want to know that you have a variety of interests that will keep your motivation high, and reduce the risk of burnout, if appointed to an AFP position.

14) What are your top three skills?

This question is assessing your understanding of the skills required in a doctor and an academic, and your suitability based on those skills. In other words, think of all the different skills you have that enable you to be a good clinical-academic, and then pick the three skills that most easily demonstrate these. Ensure that you provide evidence and state how these skills will help you achieve your ambitions.

A Bad Response:

I am a brilliantly talented pianist and performed my first solo concert at the age of 15, and so I would have to say that is my number one skill. In aiming for a dream to becoming a concert pianist and a doctor, I have had to remain extremely motivated in order to fit in rehearsal time with my clinical training, I would, therefore, rank my time management as another one of my top skills. I also enjoy musical composition and have received high praise for my work so I would rank my creativity as my third most impressive skill.

Response Analysis:

Whilst this answer demonstrates some remarkable achievements, including skills that are useful as a doctor, it seems to miss the point of the question by solely discussing the candidate's passion for music. It does provide good evidence to back up the candidate's claims, but it should explain why these skills are useful in medicine.

A Good Response:

I would say my top three skills are my communication skills, my interpersonal skills, and my ability to work under pressure. These skills perfectly fit into my desire to achieve an education-themed AFP. I have demonstrated and developed excellent communication skills through the mentoring system in University in which I provide extra teaching sessions for struggling younger students. This work has helped me to develop my patience, my ability to explain things in a simple way, my ability to understand the concerns of others, and my ability to build a rapport quickly with students who are sometimes nervous and intimidated. These skills are directly transferable to the medical consultation in which doctors must be able to put patients at ease and explain scientific concepts in simple language, and have helped further improve my teaching skills.

I have always considered myself a people person and show a range of important interpersonal skills. I take interest in other people and find it easy to be empathetic. I interact confidently with people from lots of different backgrounds. I have further developed these skills during my time in medical school where I enjoy engaging with patients. I have become a better listener in particular from this experience. Again, these skills are vital for a doctor and will help me to treat patients holistically rather than just treating their disease. Finally, through my years on the debating team, I have improved my ability to work under pressure and am confident in making decisions quickly and effectively. This skill is of vital importance when treating patients in an emergency and allows me to keep a cool head in stressful situations.

Response Analysis:

This is an excellent answer that shows a clear understanding of the skills required to be effective both as a clinician and an academic. It promotes the candidate's suitability by providing convincing evidence that the candidate possesses these skills and that they can demonstrate the practical benefits of honing these skills.

Overall:

If you are lucky enough to be asked an open-ended question like this, make sure you take full advantage of it. These types of questions give you huge freedom to display your understanding of the qualities required by a clinical-academic, and give you an invaluable opportunity to sell yourself to the interviewer. Make sure you back up everything you say with evidence and continually demonstrate why your skill-set would make you an excellent AFP trainee.

STATION 2: CLINICAL STATION

For many, one of the most daunting aspects of the AFP interview is the medical case scenario. They may feel concerned about the prospect of being asked about a medical condition that they don't know the treatment of, or being asked about a diagnostic test they are not familiar with. You should not be concerned! You are at a stage of your medical school career where you will have gained all the required knowledge to be successful in this part of the interview. The most important thing is to ensure you stick to the structure of what you would do in that specific clinical scenario.

As mentioned, the AFP interview takes different forms in different deaneries. You may, therefore, have a separate clinical scenario station and be given a sheet of paper with information about the scenario before entering the interview. Alternatively, you may be provided with this information – either in written format or verbally – naturally during the interview itself. The interviewers will ask a range of questions about how you would manage the scenario, and then may ask some more in depth questions throughout the station.

This station can also focus on clinical communication skills. Therefore, there may well be a component of the case introduced later (e.g. an angry relative), or sometimes a separate short case, where the examiners will directly ask you questions designed to test your communication skills. Finally, the interviewers may also choose to bring up an ethical or professional dilemma or scenario where they want to see if you have the required understanding of medical ethics and law, and the required professionalism skillset.

This chapter will cover how to deal with this part of the interview, including the important principles to ensure you cover, and then turn to a discussion of the common medical presentations that are discussed in the interview. Finally, we will turn to a discussion of the communication skills questions and ethical/professionalism scenario that may feature as part of the interview.

Answering the Medical Scenario

Any clinical scenario can be answered following a set of principles, which ensure patient safety. We discuss these principles now.

A typical case as given in a medical interview will explain your role (Foundation Doctor), the location (often the Medical Admissions Unit, wards or the Accident and Emergency Department), and a brief history of the patient's presentation. You will then be expected to talk through the scenario with the interviewers, who may in turn provide you with further information as you request it (e.g. blood test results). The key to success is to talk the examiners through the case as you would tackle it in real life, making sure to highlight to the examiner when you feel there are actions you need to take to preserve patient safety.

There are several main areas where you need to highlight this awareness of patient safety as a central them. They are:

1. When first seeing the patient, it is important to state that you would perform a full **ABCDE examination**, and **assess the patient's observations**, so you have an idea if the patient is in immediate danger of acute deterioration
2. If you are concerned with the patient's condition – for example, cannot obtain a pulse – then you should refer to your **Basic Life Support** knowledge
3. If you have performed the initial assessment and management and are still struggling with the patient's condition, it is essential to **escalate early to a senior** (your SHO/Registrar/ITU/Anaesthetist) if you are concerned that the patient needs reviewing by a senior clinician

A flowchart showing the key things to cover when answering a clinical scenario can be seen on the next page.

If you follow the principles as laid out, and work through the case in a logical manner, then you will be successful in the clinical scenario section of the interview.

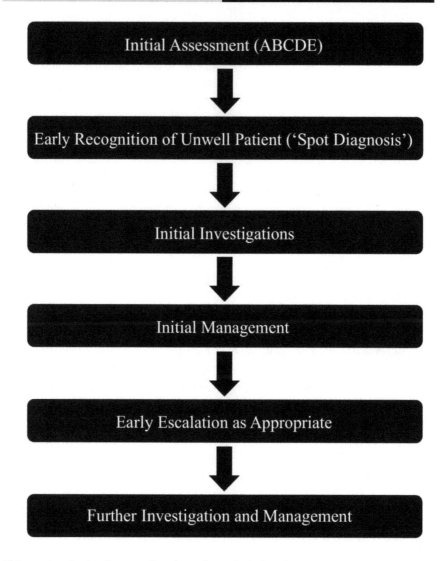

If the patient is clearly unwell and requires admission then you are going to have to tell someone; it doesn't happen magically. The **bed managers** are who you would contact to arrange admission (though you would likely be doing this only after a discussion with a senior). The interviewers may well want to know that you know what you need to do in order to admit someone from Accident and Emergency or the Outpatient Department.

Example Station 2 Interview

In the first scenario we will lay the discussion out as if it were the actual experience of one candidate sitting through this interview station. We will annotate the answer to highlight important components that satisfy the principles as discussed above. We hope this will give you an idea of how the scenarios are likely to appear in the interview itself. We will then adopt a briefer format for the following scenarios.

Scenario 1:

Scenario: You are the FY1 doctor on call, and have been asked to see Miss Price in the Medical Assessment Unit. Miss Price is an 18 year old lady who was found by her boyfriend in her bathroom, deeply asleep. Next to her were an empty half-bottle of vodka, and several empty paracetamol tablets. The boyfriend put them straight in the bin and isn't sure how much she took, but he said he thinks that she didn't take anything else. Her observations on arrival are: HR 73, BP 108/72, Sats 95%, RR 12, Temp 37.1.

Interviewer: Welcome, please have a seat.

Candidate: *Thank you, it is nice to meet you.*

Interviewer: And you. Have you had a chance to look at the scenario? Would you like to talk us through how you would approach this case?

Candidate: *Yes, I have indeed. Reading the scenario, the first thing I am concerned about is what the clinical situation is at this moment in time: I want to know her GCS and what her observations are to ensure she is stable as it sounds like she is extremely drowsy, and potentially unconscious. As such, on my arrival I would perform a full A through E assessment, and would request an up-to-date set of observations be performed. If I was concerned about the patient's GCS and observations then I would request early input from the anaesthetists and intensive care physicians, as well as my senior.*

Once I established that the patient was in a stable condition, I would attempt to take a full history from the patient, though I realise in this scenario this may be challenging. If she was awake enough to engage with me then important initial questions to ask would be exactly when she took the overdose, how many tablets she took, whether she took anything other than paracetamol (including confirming the volume of alcohol consumed), whether she has any allergies and details about her

Past Medical History. I would also want to discuss the episode in more detail, such as what caused her to do this, whether she had planned it or left a note, and whether she is pleased that she is now in hospital, as this will allow for assessment of future risk. If I could not get much of a history from the patient then it would be important to perform an early collateral history.

I would then turn to investigations: I would request an ECG to be performed, and would perform a full set of bloods including FBC, U&Es, LFTs, a clotting screen, and paracetamol and salicylate levels. I would also perform a blood gas. Depending on the results of these investigations I would initiate treatment with N-Acetyl Cysteine, and any further treatment as indicated by the history.

Interviewer: OK thank you for that, we'll break it down a little and ask some more questions. You performed an initial assessment of the patient's GCS. How would you go about doing this?

Candidate: *The Glasgow Coma Score is a 15 point score that was designed to assess patients' level of responsiveness post head injury, and therefore is an important way we can characterise the level of consciousness. 6 points are granted for motor responses (for example, whether they can obey commands), 5 points for verbal queues (for example whether they are speaking in full sentences), and 4 points on the patient's eyes (for example whether they are spontaneously open). I am concerned whenever the patient's GCS is not 15, however once the GCS drops by several points I have a very low threshold for escalation.*

Interviewer: The patient's GCS is 8. What would you do now?

Candidate: *I would perform an immediate A through E assessment, being particularly concerned about the patient's airway. If they were not maintaining their airway then I would employ different airway adjuncts as required – such as nasopharyngeal airways – until I could secure an airway. If I were not able to secure an airway and the patient were not breathing then I would put out an arrest call.*

Interviewer: You mentioned that you wanted to perform blood tests, and you mentioned which tests you wanted to perform. What in particular are you looking for in the results?

Candidate: *The blood tests are important for assessing the level of liver damage. These results include an INR, the creatinine and the arterial pH.*

The paracetamol level will allow me to work out where the patient is on the treatment line in terms of requiring treatment with N-Acetyl Cysteine. Based on the time of onset and paracetamol level measured, I would determine if she would satisfy criteria for treatment. If she did, then I would initiate a NAC infusion, which consists of three bags over a period of about 16 hours.

Interviewer: What would you do after the infusion?

Candidate: *I would repeat the blood tests mentioned above, particularly focusing on the U&Es, clotting and arterial pH. I would do this because it is at this stage where if the patient has not responded well then she may consider escalation to intensive care or even with the local liver transplant unit.*

Interviewer: Here are the results: what would you do in this situation?

RESULTS:

Hb – 142 g/L	(115 – 165 g/L)
WCC – 7 x10^9/L	(4 – 11 x10^9/L)
Plt – 193 x10^9/L	(150 – 450 x10^9/L)
Na – 138 mmol/L	(133 – 146 mmol/L)
K - 4.8 mmol/L	(3.5 – 5.3 mmol/L)
Ur - 2.5 mmol/L	(2.5 – 7.8 mmol/L)
Cr – 64 mmol/L	(59 – 104 mmol/L)
ALT – 30 iU/L	(<33 iU/L)
ALP – 53 iU/L	(30 – 130 iU/L)
INR - 1.6	
Arterial pH - 7.38	

Candidate: *I would always ensure I followed my local Trust's protocol to make sure I had the values correct, but the main ones I need to confirm are the Creatinine, INR and arterial pH. If the creatinine is greater than 300, if the INR is greater than 6.5, or if the arterial pH is <7.3 then I would immediately call the transplant unit to begin discussions, as well as discuss with my local intensive care department. In addition, the presence of serious hepatic encephalopathy is another indicator of liver damage, and would also prompt discussion with the liver unit. However, in this case I am happy that the bloods are stable and so would proceed with treatment as I mentioned earlier.*

Interviewer: You mentioned using the local protocols to find out information about treatment guidelines. Where would you find this information?

Candidate: *I would find this information in the relevant sections of my Trust's intranet.*

Interviewer: You've told me that the patient's post-NAC bloods are stable. Is there anything else you would do prior to discharging the patient?

Candidate: *Absolutely. I would review this case with a senior. I would also ensure that an early referral was sent to the Mental Health Liaison Team, and that the patient was assessed by them prior to her discharge. This, and the answers to the questions I mentioned above, is important in risk-stratifying the patient to determine the risk of her attempting to do this again soon. We would want this to be as low as possible – with arrangements put in place in the community if not – prior to discharge.*

Interviewer: It is now 6 hours later on in the shift, and the patient's mother accosts you in the corridor, demanding to know why you are keeping her daughter in hospital. How would you handle this situation?

Candidate: *I would first explain that I understand that she must be concerned, but explain that the corridor is not the best place to have these discussions and that the best thing to do would be to have a private discussion in one of the relatives rooms, if she agreed to it.*

Once we were in this room I would explain that I am unable to give confidential information to the mother without first getting permission from the patient.

Interviewer: The mum interrupts you here and says she and her daughter have a very understanding and open relationship, and explains that she knows the daughter would want her to know what is going on.

Candidate: *I would apologise and say that I have to respect the right to confidentiality of my patients, but if she would give me a moment I could potentially ask her daughter if she would be willing for me to discuss her case with her mother. If the daughter gave me permission then I would go through the information with the mother, but if the daughter refused then I would have to apologise to the mother and explain that I am unable to provide her with further information.*

Interviewer: Later in the shift, about 8 hours into the infusion, the patient becomes quite agitated and disconnects the NAC and is telling the nurses she is insisting on leaving. The nurse runs to you and asks you to speak to the patient. What would you do now?

Candidate: *I would go speak to the patient and first ask her if there is anything I can provide that will help her to relax, such as a cup of tea. I would try to explain that I understand that it is very frustrated staying in hospital, and I would then ask for her understanding of the situation and why she needed treatment. I would explain that if she did not receive treatment then this was a potentially life-threatening disease, which could lead to liver failure, and in turn if that was not treated then she could die.*

I would explain that she needs to finish the rest of her infusion, and to have the post NAC bloods prior to discharge, because if she doesn't she risks causing permanent damage to her liver, and potentially even death.

Interviewer: The patient understands this, as she hadn't had this explained to her before. She elects to stay for the end of her treatment. Thank you for your answers. That concludes the clinical station.

Candidate: *Thank you for the opportunity.*

Analysis: The candidate does well here. They appropriately assess the patient initially, performing GCS and ABCDE assessments in a timely fashion. They correctly investigate and manage the patient, and understand the King's College criteria for liver transplant referral. In addition, the candidate handles well the communication skills section of the station, dealing with the request of the relative and also of the patient's request to leave very professionally.

Scenario 2:

Scenario: You are the FY2 on-call for General Surgery, and have been asked to see Miss Jones in the Emergency Department. Miss Jones is a 20 year old lady who has presented with a 2 day history of migratory right iliac fossa pain of increasing severity. Her observations on arrival are: HR 95, BP 108/72, Sats 100% on air, RR 16, Temp 38.1

Interviewer: Welcome, please have a seat.

Candidate: *Thank you.*

Interviewer: Have you had a chance to look at the scenario? Would you like to talk us through how you would approach this case?

Candidate: *Yes, I have. I would manage this patient using an ABCDE approach and following ALS protocols. I will ensure her airway is patent, check oxygen saturations using a pulse oximeter and administer oxygen if required. I will measure her respiratory rate, obtain a blood pressure reading and measure her heart rate. I will ensure she has wide-bore IV access and obtain bloods to check full blood count, urea and electrolytes, c-reactive protein, liver function tests, clotting profile, group and screen and a venous blood gas. Given that she is febrile, I will use this opportunity to take blood cultures. I will commence intravenous fluid resuscitation with a litre of warm crystalloid. I will formally assess her GCS and check her blood glucose levels. I would also request a urine sample to dip and perform a urinary pregnancy test on.*

This patient is fulfilling criteria consistent with sepsis. Therefore, it is important I follow the 'sepsis 6.' This would involve administering intravenous (IV) broad-spectrum antibiotics, IV fluids, high flow oxygen depending on saturations, and taking blood cultures, an arterial blood gas to measure lactate, and inserting a urinary catheter to measure urine output.

Once I have established that the patient was in a stable condition, I would take undertake a full history from the patient, and examination. Once her drug history and allergies are known, I would prescribe appropriate analgesia following the WHO analgesia ladder.

Interviewer: OK thank you for that, we'll break it down a little and ask some more questions. Given her age, what of the tests you have listed already, would you say is the most important?

Candidate: *Given that she is a female of child-bearing age, she should have a urinary pregnancy test to rule out pregnancy and an ectopic pregnancy. I would also take a gynaecological history as part of my work-up.*

Interviewer: Thank you. What differentials would you consider at this stage?

Candidate: *My differentials can be divided into surgical (acute appendicitis, an inflamed Meckel's diverticulum, diverticulitis), urological (ureteric or bladder calculi), gynaecological (an ectopic pregnancy which may have ruptured, (if positive pregnancy test), salpingitis, pelvic inflammatory disease) and medical (mesenteric adenitis, urinary tract infection and gastroenteritis).*

Interviewer: Let's say that her blood tests and urine dip have now come back. She has a white cell count of 16, CRP of 40, and urine dip as well pregnancy tests are negative, and you have a strong feeling that she has acute appendicitis. What would you do next?

Candidate: *I would admit this patient, ensure she has been started on IV antibiotics, keep her nil by mouth, and inform my registrar of my suspicion. I would also ensure the patient is kept up to date and that my thoughts about her diagnosis have been explained to her.*

Interviewer: Your registrar reviews the patient and agrees with your diagnosis of acute appendicitis. He asks you to prepare the patient for theatre. Apart from informing theatre staff, what else do you need to do?

Candidate: *In order to prepare this patient for theatre, I need to ensure her clotting profile has been reviewed, her group and save has been processed and that there is blood available for her should she require it. I will need to ensure the consent process for laparoscopic appendicectomy has been performed, and will discuss with my seniors to ensure that is completed. I will also need to inform the on-call Anaesthetist, book the patient for theatre and inform theatre staff.*

Interviewer: Are you going to consent the patient yourself?

Candidate: *As I am not fully aware of the intricacies of the procedure, neither am I capable of performing the procedure, I would not consent this patient myself. I would inform my registrar and ask if I could watch them consent the patient. I would like to use this as a learning opportunity so during a future opportunity, I could potentially consent the patient.*

Interviewer: What antibiotics will you start her on?

Candidate: *I would commence broad-spectrum IV antibiotics as per trust guidelines, and taking into account any allergies she may have.*

Interviewer: What are the possible locations of the appendix?

Candidate: *The appendix can have a number of possible locations. The commonest is retrocaecal, however it can also be pelvic, retrocolic, and pre-ileal.*

Interviewer: What is a Meckel's diverticulum?

Candidate: *This is an embryological remnant of the vitello-intestinal duct. Statistically, it is found in 2% of the population, is twice as common in men than women, is found 2ft proximal to the ileocaecal valve and is 2" long. Complications including bleeding and diverticulitis.*

Interviewer: What are some of the main points of post-operative care?

Candidate: *There are a number of important issues regarding this patient's post-operative care. These include adequate analgesia, fluids, nutrition, mobilising as tolerated to reduce the risk of a venous thromboembolism, and if required, antibiotics based on the findings during appendicectomy.*

Interviewer: Thank you, that concludes the clinical station.

Candidate: *Thank you for the opportunity.*

Analysis: The candidate does well here. They appropriately assess the patient initially, performing an ABCDE assessments in a timely fashion. They correctly investigate and manage the patient, including instigating the 'sepsis 6.' They present a wide-range of sensible differentials, and recognise the importance of gynaecological pathology. Escalating appropriately and being aware of the principles of post-operative care are highlighted here.

Example Medical Cases

For the remainder of this chapter we will focus on some of the other common cases that can come up during in the interview. We'll cover these as if the candidate were giving one long answer, and include the key points in their answer, but as you've seen above the interviewers will interrupt and steer the interview as they see fit.

Scenario 3:

A 25 year old male with depression self-presents after taking an overdose of multiple medications. He reports he has taken sertraline, iron supplements and aspirin. He is unsure of the exact quantities because he had alcohol at the same time. You are an FY1 doctor on the clerking team, and have been asked to see the patient and determine the next steps.

Interviewer: How would you approach this scenario?

Answer: *On arrival to this patient I would perform a full ABCDE assessment. Having established this was stable I would commence with a more detailed history. I would try to establish just how many of each medication he took. I would need to establish exactly when he took the overdose. If he were able to discuss it, I would need to discuss the circumstances that led him to taking the overdose and how he feels now that he is in the hospital. I would also want to establish risk of further attempts, including if he wrote a note, if he made efforts not to be found, and if he drank alcohol with the attempt. I would perform a full examination of the patient, including cardiovascular and neurological.*

I would request a full set of observations, an ECG, gain IV access, and would send blood tests for analysis including FBC, U&Es, LFTs, CRP, clotting, paracetamol levels, aspirin levels and iron levels. I would also consult with Toxbase to find out what the protocol is for management of the different overdoses that the patient has consumed: I would want to confirm with Toxbase but I understand that there is risk of cardiac events and the development of serotonin syndrome with sertraline overdoses, risk of gastrointestinal effects and liver failure with iron overdoses, and risk of tinnitus, drowsiness and coma with aspirin overdoses.

Interviewer: Here are some of the investigation results: what is your interpretation of them?

RESULTS:

Hb – 145 g/L	(130 – 180 g/L)
WCC – 10 x10⁹/L	(4 – 11 x10⁹/L)
Plt – 294 x10⁹/L	(150 – 450 x10⁹/L)

Hb – 145 g/L   *(130 – 180 g/L)*
WCC – 10 $x10^9$/L   *(4 – 11 $x10^9$/L)*
Plt – 294 $x10^9$/L   *(150 – 450 $x10^9$/L)*

Na – 135 mmol/L   *(133 – 146 mmol/L)*
K – 4.9 mmol/L   *(3.5 – 5.3 mmol/L)*
Ur – 4.1 mmol/L   *(2.5 – 7.8 mmol/L)*
Cr – 76 mmol/L   *(59 – 104 mmol/L)*

ALT – 32 iU/L   *(<33 iU/L)*
ALP – 87 iU/L   *(30 – 130 iU/L)*

CRP – 6 mg/L   *(<5 mg/L)*

INR – 1.1

Paracetamol level – <5 mg/L
Aspirin level – 34 mg/dL
Iron Level – 200 mcg/dL

Answer: *The blood results suggest confirm that the patient has indeed had an overdose of aspirin and iron. The paracetamol levels, however, are normal, and the FBC, U&Es and LFTs are unremarkable. I do not think the CRP is significantly raised, but this would be important to keep an eye on with repeat blood tests.*

Interviewer: What would your next course of action be?

Answer: *I would ensure that the patient has aggressive fluid resuscitation running. I would arrange for their admission to a bed with a cardiac monitor. Because I am somewhat unsure of the levels of iron following an overdose, and because this overdose has involved multiple medications including sertraline, I would contact toxbase to confirm my management plan with them and see if they had any specific further advice. I would arrange for repeat blood tests in a few hours to ensure that the iron levels are falling, and would also request a further ECG to ensure the QTc remains stable.*

In addition, I would ensure that the mental health liason team were contacted to review the patient prior to discharge, and I would ensure that I discussed the case with my senior if I had concerns about this.

Analysis: The candidate has a safe approach to this patient. They perform an initial assessment to ensure the patient isn't acutely unwell, and then begin further assessment and investigation. They also show that they know what to do in these circumstance and work within their professional limits: both by stating that they would discuss with a senior but importantly also by saying that they would look the case up on Toxbase.

Top Tip! Toxbase: this is an incredibly useful resource when dealing with complex overdoses. The website provides the common symptoms and effects of overdosing on a wide variety of medications. In complex cases, it is possible to contact pharmacologists through Toxbase's telephone service and consult with someone who has experience with managing the particular overdose. Each Trust has its unique logon details, and this is something you should ensure you are familiar with in new hospital that you work in!

Scenario 4:

A 21 year old female patient is admitted to Acute Medical Unit having been found confused at home by her flatmate. She is pyrexial on admission, and her admission observations are as follows: HR 89, BP 88/54, Sats 97%, RR 16, Temp 39. During her stay her GCS begins to drop and she becomes increasingly drowsy. You are the FY1 doctor and are asked to urgently review this patient.

Interviewer: How would you approach this scenario?

Answer: *On arrival to this patient I would ensure that I perform a full A to E assessment. I am quite concerned about her airway due to her low GCS, and am also concerned about her haemodynamic status along with pyrexia, and am concerned that she is septic.*

Therefore, my initial course of action would be to ensure that her airway was stable and protected, and that we had two large bore cannulas for IV access. I would ensure that FBC, U&Es, CRP, lactate, clotting and group and save blood tests were sent. I would also ensure blood cultures were sent at this stage. I would also ensure that I got a 500ml fluid challenge running to observe if her blood pressure responds to this. She should also have a catheter inserted and oxygen administered as part of the 'Sepsis 6' bundle.

Following these interventions, I would let my seniors know about this patient and would commence more of a thorough history (collateral, if available), and would perform a full examination. In particular, I would want to ensure there is no focal neurology and would want to perform fundoscopy.

Interviewer: Here are some of the investigation results: what is your interpretation of them?

RESULTS:

Hb – 120 g/L	*(115 – 165 g/L)*
WCC – 22 x10⁹/L	*(4 – 11 x10⁹/L)*
Plt – 256 x10⁹/L	*(150 – 450 x10⁹/L)*
Na – 139 mmol/L	*(133 – 146 mmol/L)*
K – 3.8 mmol/L	*(3.5 – 5.3 mmol/L)*
Ur – 3.2 mmol/L	*(2.5 – 7.8 mmol/L)*
Cr – 69 mmol/L	*(59 – 104 mmol/L)*
CRP – 189 mg/L	*(<5 mg/L)*
INR – 1.0	

Answer: *The blood results suggest an infective picture in this case. The haemoglobin is normal but the white cell count is significantly raised. In addition, the CRP is significantly elevated, again suggesting a picture of an active immune response. The U&Es and clotting are normal, and therefore the bloods taken together with the presentation with acute deterioration and pyrexia are consistent with an acute infection. Given the history, I am concerned about the possibility of meningitis. I would want an LP as a matter of urgency, and if this was unavailable I would treat empirically.*

Interviewer: Here are the CSF Analysis results. How would you interpret them?

CSF Analysis RESULTS:

Red Blood Cells – 8 /mm³   *(0 – 10 /mm³)*

WCC – 124 /mm³   *(0 – 5 /mm³)*
Neutrophil % – 82%
Lymphocyte % – 18%

Protein – 0.54 g/L   *(0.15 – 0.45 g/L)*

Glucose – 2.4 mmol/L   *(2.8 – 4.2 mmol/L)*

Opening Pressure – 25 cm H₂0   *(10 – 20 cm H₂0)*

Answer: Immediately, these results suggest to me that the patient is suffering with bacterial meningitis. The white blood cells are raised with a neutrophilia, the protein is raised and the glucose is low. In addition, the opening pressure is raised. All of these findings suggest to me that the patient has bacterial meningitis.

Interviewer: What would your next course of action be?

Answer: *Given the blood and CSF results along with the pyrexia, the likely diagnosis is bacterial meningitis. Therefore I discuss this early with a senior doctor, and would prescribe empirical antibiotics therapy (ceftriaxone). I would also ensure good supportive management was in place such as sufficient intravenous fluid rehydration.*

If the patient was not improving or responding to fluid challenges then I would further escalate this by contacting the intensive care team.

Analysis: The candidate once performs the correct initial assessment of the patient and instigates appropriate initial therapy with empirical antibiotics and fluid challenges after appropriate discussion with their senior. The investigations they request are appropriate (with the cultures being especially important in a potentially infective presentations), and they identify the potential need for a lumbar puncture in this case. They also explain that they would not delay in escalating this case if the patient did not respond sufficiently.

Scenario 5:

Top Tip! You may be expected to talk the examiners through a set of CSF fluid analysis results. Take the following as an example:

WCC: Elevated, 75% lymphocytes   **Protein:** Low
Glucose (CSF:Serum ratio): Normal

What do you think the likely diagnosis is in this case?

The high lymphocyte count along with low protein indicate that a bacterial meningitis is not likely. This picture could represent viral meningitis, or may represent tuberculous meningitis: an important diagnosis not to forget. Make sure you are familiar with other presentations of CSF fluid (tuberculosis, bacterial, viral infections etc) prior to the interview so that you can talk the examiners through the CSF analysis with confidence.

A 72 year old lady is brought in to the emergency department via ambulance following a fall at home. On examination, she is unable to weight bear, and her left leg is shortened and externally rotated. She has a past medical history of hypertension, hypercholesterolaemia and type 2 diabetes. You are the FY2 doctor on-call for trauma and orthopaedics and have been bleeped by the emergency department. No X-Rays have been taken just yet.

Interviewer: How would you approach this scenario?

Answer: *I would perform a full ABCDE assessment following ALS protocols. I will ensure her airway is patent, check oxygen saturations using a pulse oximeter and administer oxygen if required. I will ensure her c-spine is stable. I will measure her respiratory rate, obtain a blood pressure reading and measure her heart rate. I will ensure she has wide-bore IV access and obtain bloods to check full blood count, urea and electrolytes, c-reactive protein, clotting profile, group and screen and a venous blood gas. I will commence intravenous fluid resuscitation with a litre of warm crystalloid. I will then formally assess her GCS and check her blood glucose level.*

When I am confident she has been stabilised, I will prescribe analgesia as required following the WHO analgesic ladder, and taking into account any allergies.

I will then perform a full systems examination. I will ensure I examine both legs, as well as the joint above and below the joint in question, in this case her knees and lumbar spine.

Interviewer: What imaging would you request?

Answer: *She will need X-Rays of the pelvis and left hip in antero-posterior, as well as lateral views to look for a fracture.*

Interviewer: Let's say her X-Ray shows an intracapsular neck of femur fracture. How would you manage her next?

Answer: *She requires admission to fix the fracture. I will escalate this with my senior to ensure that the patient has received appropriate analgesia, has been consented, and has had the appropriate pre-theatre workup performed.*

Interviewer: You are called to review her on the ward 2 days post-op as the nursing staff are concerned that she has become acutely short of breath and hypoxic. What are your differentials?

Answer: *Given that she has had recent surgery and is likely to have reduced mobility, my top differential is a pulmonary embolism from a deep vein thrombosis. My other differentials include a hospital acquired pneumonia and heart failure. I would perform a full ABCDE assessment, my investigations would include a chest x-ray, an arterial blood gas and a full set of bloods including FBC, U&Es, and CRP. D-Dimer would be of limited use given her recent surgery. She should undergo a CT pulmonary angiogram to identify a pulmonary embolism. I would also inform my senior of my suspicions and if I felt there was strong evidence from her investigations to suggest a P/E, I would initiate treatment-dose low molecular weight heparin based on her body weight while awaiting the CT pulmonary angiogram.*

Analysis: The candidate once performs the correct initial assessment of the patient and requests appropriate imaging. They show understanding of the potential post-operative complications that can occur such as a pulmonary embolism and HAP.

Scenario 6:

A 47 year old patient on the gastroenterology ward has started vomiting copious amounts of fresh red blood. His observations are: HR 99, BP 90/60, Sats 98%, RR 16, and his Hb was 85 when taken on the morning blood round. You, as the FY1 doctor on call, have been asked to see him urgently as the nursing staff are very concerned about him.

Interviewer: How would you approach this scenario?

Answer: *This patient's condition sounds very concerning, and so I would prioritise seeing this patient as soon as possible. On arrival, should it be obvious that he was continuing to vomit blood, I would initiate the major haemorrhage protocol and perform a full ABCDE assessment of the patient. I would want to ensure that the patient was maintaining his airway, as well as confirming that there were no other sources of bleeding.*

As long as the patient's airway was secure, I would immediately commence blood transfusions plus giving boluses of intravenous fluids due to his haemodynamic status in an attempt to resuscitate him. I would ensure that two independent Group and Save blood samples were sent for further cross-match testing in case more blood is needed after the initial protocol. During this time I would ensure a full set of repeat bloods had been sent: FBC, U&Es, LFTs and a clotting screen.

I would also call my senior and request that they review the patient early, as well as contact the gastroenterology team and the intensive care team due to the severity of his condition.

Whilst waiting for my seniors to arrive, and once the blood was up and running, I would begin investigating the patient's medical background (through questioning and the patient's notes). I would attempt to ascertain a cause for the bleeding: for example, if he was known to suffer from cirrhosis then this may be a variceal bleed.

Interviewer: Here are some of the investigation results: what is your interpretation of them?

RESULTS:

Hb – 55 g/L	*(130 – 180 g/L)*
WCC – 5.3 x10⁹/L	*(4 – 11 x10⁹/L)*
Plt – 165 x10⁹/L	*(150 – 450 x10⁹/L)*
Na – 143 mmol/L	*(133 – 146 mmol/L)*
K – 4.5 mmol/L	*(3.5 – 5.3 mmol/L)*
Ur – 12.3 mmol/L	*(2.5 – 7.8 mmol/L)*
Cr – 69 mmol/L	*(59 – 104 mmol/L)*
ALT – 54 iU/L	*(<33 iU/L)*
ALP – 78 iU/L	*(30 – 130 iU/L)*
INR – 2.8	

Answer: *There are several things that are concerning in this picture. The first is the low haemoglobin. This does suggest that the bleeding is significant, and re-confirms the requirement for urgent blood transfusions. I am concerned that the urea is raised: this suggests that the patient has swallowed a significant amount of blood and therefore this bleed likely represents an upper GI bleed. The raised INR suggests that the patient has a coagulopathy, and putting this all together, along with the slightly raised ALT, my initial concerns is that the patient has an element of chronic liver disease.*

Interviewer: What would your next course of action be?

Answer: *I would continue with the blood transfusions. After discussion with a senior, I would consider prescribing 10mg IV Vitamin K in an attempt to resolve the coagulopathy. Should the patient continue to vomit, terlipressin may be indicated, although I would confirm this with the gastroenterology team. In addition, it appears that urgent endoscopy will be required, and this would be another reason that I would be contacting the gastroenterology team as a matter of urgency.*

Analysis: The candidate swiftly realised the urgency of the situation, and they communicated this to the interviewers well. They indicated they would perform a full A to E assessment in this patient, but importantly acknowledged that they may initiate the Major Haemorrhage Protocol (MHP) before this full assessment. Candidates shouldn't be afraid to do this: if it is obvious that the patient is haemodynamically compromised (as in this scenario) and actively vomiting blood, then the ABCDE assessment from the end of the bed is obvious enough, and the MHP can and should be triggered early.

Other important and successful points in this scenario are the early involvement of seniors and of the other important clinical teams: gastroenterology and intensive care medicine. They talked about the important investigations to perform: the full set of bloods along with the endoscopy. The candidate also found the clues in the bloods appropriately – the haemoglobin is obvious enough, but it was important to pick up on the raised urea and clotting abnormality.

Top Tip! The Major Haemorrhage Protocol is a rapid way of obtaining blood products in an emergency. Though there may be variations in individual Trusts, the main products included are:
- 4 Units of RBCs (Universal Donor: O negative)
- 4 Units of Fresh Frozen Plasma

Scenario 7:

A 47 year old lady has undergone a laparoscopic cholecystectomy for acute calculous cholecystitis. The operation was successfully completed and a drain was left at the gallbladder bed due to some bleeding encountered as the gallbladder was dissected off its fossa. You, as the FY1 on call for ward cover, are called to see her 1 day post-op as she has spiked a fever of 38.7°C, there appears to be a dark green fluid in her drain and she is starting to feel unwell.

Interviewer: How would you approach this scenario?

Answer: *On arrival to this patient I would ensure that I perform a full A to E assessment as per ALS protocols. I will ensure she has wide-bore IV access and a full set of observations. I will take a set of blood tests and blood cultures, these will include an FBC, Urea and Electrolytes, CRP and Liver Function Tests.*

I will ensure this patient has adequate intravenous fluid resuscitation if required, before taking a history and performing a full systems examination to identify the cause of the fever.

Interviewer: What are the possible causes of fever in this patient?

Answer: *There are a number of possible causes of fever in this patient. These include a hospital acquired pneumonia, wound infection, post-operative collections, bile leak and urinary tract infection. To investigate for these alongside a full systems examination, she should have a chest x-ray to look for a consolidation, wound swabs if there is evidence of wound infection, urine dip and if she has a urinary catheter, a sample should be sent for microscopy, culture and sensitivities. She should be commenced on IV antibiotics as per trust guidelines once the source of the fever is identified.*

Interviewer: Given the appearance of the drain output, what are you most concerned about?

Answer: *I am most concerned about a bile leak.*

Interviewer: How would you manage a suspected bile leak?

Answer: *She should undergo a contrast CT scan of the abdomen and pelvis to look for a bile leak. If there is confirmed bile leak, one management option is to insert a biliary stent via ERCP to stop further bile leak. For an ERCP, I would contact the Gastroenterologists. Another option is to take the patient back to theatre for a laparoscopic washout.*

Analysis: The candidate performs the correct initial assessment of the patient and states a good range of possible sources of the pyrexia. They understand that a bile leak is a likely complication given the appearance of the drain fluid and are aware of the some of the principles of managing this. This also shows the involvement of other teams, and how important it is to know who to contact for help. Apart from this, they also mentioned important investigations that would help rule out other causes of fever in the post-op patient.

Scenario 8:

A 57 year old man is admitted with what he describes as the worst headache he has ever experienced. His observations on arrival are: HR 64, BP 130/92, Sats 98%, RR 16, Temp 36.9. During assessment in the A&E department his GCS begins to drop. You are the FY1 doctor and have been asked to see this patient as you registrar is currently dealing with a Major Trauma.

Interviewer: How would you approach this scenario?

Answer: *I am concerned in this patient about the possibility of a subarachnoid haemorrhage. I would perform a full A to E assessment on arrival to this patient. Following this, I would perform a full history and examination, paying close attention to the Neurological examination to identify any clinical signs. It sounds as if the patient's GCS is starting to drop, and so this is very concerning. I would ensure that he has a stable airway, using adjuncts as necessary, and then would contact my senior urgently to inform them of the situation. I would also discuss the patient early with the neurology and neurosurgery team, as well as potentially the anaesthetists and intensive care team if I was concerned about preserving the patient's airway.*

The patient would also require additional investigation. They would need to have an ECG, a full set of blood tests (including FBC, U&Es, LFTs, CRP and clotting screen), and would also need urgent CT head imaging to be done. Depending on the results of this and the clinical suspicion of a bleed, the patient may also require lumbar puncture (sending for xanthochromia) to further investigate the possibility of a SAH.

Interviewer: Here are some of the investigation results: what is your interpretation of them?

RESULTS:

Hb – 150 g/L	(130 – 180 g/L)
WCC – 6.7 x10⁹/L	(4 – 11 x10⁹/L)
Plt – 167 x10⁹/L	(150 – 450 x10⁹/L)

Hb – 150 g/L   *(130 – 180 g/L)*
WCC – 6.7 x10^9/L   *(4 – 11 x10^9/L)*
Plt – 167 x10^9/L   *(150 – 450 x10^9/L)*

Na – 141 mmol/L   *(133 – 146 mmol/L)*
K – 3.5 mmol/L   *(3.5 – 5.3 mmol/L)*
Ur – 6.7 mmol/L   *(2.5 – 7.8 mmol/L)*
Cr – 74 mmol/L   *(59 – 104 mmol/L)*

CRP – <5 mg/L   *(<5 mg/L)*

ALT – 20 iU/L   *(<33 iU/L)*
ALP – 45 iU/L   *(30 – 130 iU/L)*

INR – 1.0

Answer: *The blood tests show normal values: this means that my suspicion of a possible sub-arachnoid haemorrhage is still quite high. The normal WCC and CRP go some way to making an infective cause of his headache (though unlikely from the history) even less likely.*

Interviewer: What would your next course of action be?

Answer: *As I mentioned earlier, I think the important next steps would be CT imaging of the patient's brain, followed by lumbar puncture looking for xanthochromia.*

I would also monitor the patient's observations for any changes: I know there is a significant risk of further bleeding if the blood pressure is too high and so I would aim to titrate the blood pressure to keep it below 140 mmHg. I would also treat the patient's pain with analgesia, if the pain was ongoing, and would monitor for seizure activity and treat as appropriate.

Analysis: The candidate correctly identifies the most serious differential diagnosis that they must rule out, and they perform the initial assessment safely. They identify that the GCS is reported to be dropping, and so realise that airway protection is going to be vital in this case. The candidate also states that they will escalate this to seniors early, as the patient has the potential to rapidly decompensate if their GCS continues to drop. The candidate shows they know the appropriate investigation (CT and LP) in these cases, but also note that it will depend on the specific clinical scenario whether and when the LP must be performed.

Top Tip! Be prepared to talk through the Glasgow Coma Scale (GCS) during the interview. This is a clinical scale developed to assess patients' level of consciousness, and so stratify seriousness of head injury. There are three components:

Eyes:	Verbal:	Motor:
4. Open	5. Conversing normally	6. Obeys commands
3. Open to voice	4. Conversing but disoriented	5. Localizes to pain
2. Open to pain	3. Inappropriate words	4. Withdraws from pain
1. Not opening	2. Incomprehensible noises	3. Abnormal flexion
	1. No sounds	2. Abnormal extension
		1. No motor response

Adding the best responses in each category gives a score from 3-15, with lower scores indicating a reduced level of consciousness

---

Scenario 9:

A 45 year old patient presents to A&E with severe right loin pain, which is colicky in nature and radiating to the right groin. He states he has noticed some light specks of blood in his urine. His observations on arrival are: HR 100, BP 105/60, Sats 99% on air, RR 20, temperature 38.9°C. His urine dip is positive for blood (+++), nitrites and leucocytes. He has been referred to you, the FY2 on-call. You have been asked to see him urgently.

Interviewer: How would you approach this scenario?

Answer: *I would manage this patient using an ABCDE approach and following ALS protocols. Given the latest set of observations, I would ensure his airway is patient, at present he does not require additional oxygen. I will auscultate his lungs and heart. I will measure his blood pressure and check his pulse. I will ensure he has wide-bore intravenous access and take a set of bloods including a venous blood gas and blood cultures. This patient will need intravenous fluid resuscitation commencing with crystalloid such as Hartman's solution. He will require a 3-way urinary catheter due to the presence of visible haematuria. Prior to insertion, I would like to send his latest urine sample to the laboratory for microscopy, culture and sensitivity. On completing this initial assessment, I would like to take a full history and perform a full systems examination; in particular an abdominal systems examination.*

Interviewer: Here are some of the results of his investigations: Hb 145, WCC 16, Plt 500, Na 149, K 4.5, Ur 20, Cr 240, CRP 148.

Answer: *His inflammatory markers raise the concern of sepsis. Given his presenting complaint and urine dip, a urinary source is the most likely. He also has deranged renal function which suggest a degree of acute kidney injury. I would cross-reference his latest urea and creatinine with any historical results to identify if there is any history of chronic kidney disease.*

Interviewer: What would your next course of action be?

Answer: *I would complete the 'sepsis 6' by commencing intravenous antibiotics, high flow oxygen if required and measuring his urine output, as the other components; blood cultures, blood gas for lactate, IV fluids and urinary catheter have already been inserted.*

Interviewer: What are your differentials?

Answer: *My main differentials are an obstructing renal calculus, pyelonephritis, lower urinary tract infection and I would also like to rule out a ruptured abdominal aortic aneurysm. I would like to request an urgent CT scan of the kidneys, ureters and bladder, after discussion with my registrat, as this is the gold standard investigation for identifying renal calculi and can also visualise the abdominal aorta.*

Interviewer: The CT KUB shows hydronephrosis of the right kidney secondary to a 7mm obstructing calculus. What would you do next?

Answer: *After review with my registrar, I would like to admit this patient under Urology. They will require urgent decompression of the obstructed system. This can be achieved via a nephrostomy or via stent insertion. I would also inform my registrar and request a senior review of this patient.*

Interviewer: What are some causes of an acute kidney injury?

Answer: *The causes of an acute kidney injury can be divided into pre-renal, renal and post-renal. Pre-renal causes include hypovolaemia leading to reduced perfusion of the kidney. This can be caused by dehydration or bleeding. Renal causes include nephrotoxic drugs such as Gentamicin and Non-steroidal anti-inflammatory drugs such as Ibuprofen and Naproxen. Post-renal causes include obstruction of the urinary tract, for example by a renal calculus in the ureter or external compression by a colonic tumour.*

Analysis: The candidate completed a thorough assessment and identified that the patient was septic, as well as what the likely source in this case was. They provided a number of relevant differentials and appropriate imaging for them, as well as awareness of the urgency of decompressing an obstructed, infected system, and early senior involvement.

Scenario 10:

A 38 year old female patient presents to the A&E department with acute abdominal pain radiating to her back and vomiting. Her HR is 94, BP 103/68, Sats 96%, RR 17 and Temp 37.3. You, the FY1 doctor, have been asked to see her.

Interviewer: How would you approach this scenario?

Answer: *I would perform a full ABCDE assessment on my arrival to this patient. Judging by the observations, one of my concerns is with the slightly low blood pressure, and with the clinical picture potentially suggestive of pancreatitis, aggressive fluid resuscitation may be important in this patient. I would prescribe a fluid bolus initially in an attempt to correct the hypotension.*

Once I was happy with the full A through E assessment I would take a full history from the patient, finding more out about the pain and vomiting. I would want to know about the patient's past medical history (including whether she has a history of gallstones), and would want to ask her questions about her alcohol consumption.

For investigations, I would want an ECG and a pregnancy test. In addition, I would request a full set of blood tests. I would request FBC, U&Es, LFTs, CRP, clotting screen, and Amylase and Lipase (if available). I would then consider requesting an abdominal ultrasound scan.

Interviewer: Here are some of the investigation results: what is your interpretation of them?

RESULTS:

Hb – 124 g/L	(115 – 165 g/L)
WCC – 12 x10⁹/L	(4 – 11 x10⁹/L)
Plt – 234 x10⁹/L	(150 – 450 x10⁹/L)
Na – 134 mmol/L	(133 – 146 mmol/L)
K – 4.2 mmol/L	(3.5 – 5.3 mmol/L)
Ur – 4.5 mmol/L	(2.5 – 7.8 mmol/L)
Cr – 81 mmol/L	(59 – 104 mmol/L)
ALT – 23 iU/L	(<33 iU/L)
ALP – 34 iU/L	(30 – 130 iU/L)
CRP – 68 mg/L	(<5 mg/L)
Amylase – 234 iU/dL	(28 –100 iU/dL)

Pregnancy Test - Negative

Answer: *The patient's U&Es and LFTs are normal. The white blood cells and CRP are raised indicating an inflammatory picture. The amylase is significantly raised, which means my initial diagnosis of pancreatitis is now extremely likely.*

Interviewer: What would your next course of action be?

Answer: *I would commence treatment with the fluid resuscitation that I mentioned earlier. I would prescribe analgesia for the patient's pain. I would provide supplemental oxygen to ensure adequate tissue oxygenation. I would also arrange an abdominal ultrasound scan.*

I would discuss the case with my senior – and if there were any signs of the patient becoming more unwell then I would have a low threshold for discussion with the intensive care team. If the patient has a strong history of gallstones or this is confirmed on imaging, then the patient may require ERCP.

Analysis: The candidate carries out a thorough initial assessment, and investigates and manages the patient appropriately. They correctly identify their main differential diagnosis. They involve their seniors at an appropriate stage, and confirm that if there is any sign of the patient deteriorating further then the patient will need to be reviewed by, and likely managed in, intensive care.

Top Tip! Risk stratification/prediction of severity can come up when discussing pancreatitis. The common scores used are the APACHE II score and the Glasgow criteria. We would recommend familiarity with at least the Glasgow criteria. They are:

- P – PaO2 < 8kPa
- A – Age > 55 years
- N – Neutrophilia (WCC > 15×10^9/L)
- C – Calcium < 2mmol/L
- R – Renal (Urea > 16mmol/L)
- E – Enzymes (LDH > 600IU/L, AST > 200IU/L)
- A – Albumin <32g/L
- S – Sugar (blood glucose > 10mmol/L)

A score of 3 or more indiciates the patient has presented with a severe episode of pancreatitis and may warrant urgent transfer to the intensive care unit.

Scenario 11:

An 18 year old female patient is admitted with acute shortness of breath. She has a background of asthma, and is noted to be struggling to complete full sentences. Her observations on arrival are: HR 80, BP 110/72, Sats 91%, RR 28, Temp 37.4. Her peak flow is 35% of her best. You are the FY1 doctor on call, and have been asked to see this patient in the Medical Assessment Unit.

Interviewer: How would you approach this scenario?

Answer: *I am worried about an acute severe exacerbation of asthma in this patient. This is suggested by the low peak flow and her inability to complete full sentences. I would immediately perform a full ABCDE assessment on the patient. I would particularly look for breathing signs during this assessment, including wheeze and a silent chest, being particularly concerned if I thought the latter were present. I would also ensure that her peak flows are re-measured at regular intervals, as if they drop under 33%, or if the patient tires further, then this would fall into the classification of life-threatening asthma attack.*

It is clear that this patient needs urgent treatment, and so I would commence back-to-back 5mg salbutamol nebulisers on oxygen, as well as commencing ipratropium nebulisers. I would follow the British Thoracic Society guidelines when escalating therapy in this patient, and I would involve my seniors early when making management decisions about escalating her therapy. Escalated options include intravenous steroid therapy, and consideration of magnesium sulphate injections.

The patient also requires investigating further, including blood tests such as an FBC and U&Es, and repeat peak flow measurements. I would also perform an Arterial Blood Gas in this patient due to her low oxygen saturation. If the patient were stable enough then I would also want a Chest X-Ray.

Interviewer: Here are some of the investigation results: what is your interpretation of them?

RESULTS:

Hb – 116 g/L	(115 – 165 g/L)
WCC – 11.2 x10⁹/L	(4 – 11 x10⁹/L)
Plt – 329 x10⁹/L	(150 – 450 x10⁹/L)
Na – 138 mmol/L	(133 – 146 mmol/L)
K – 4.9 mmol/L	(3.5 – 5.3 mmol/L)
Ur – 2.9 mmol/L	(2.5 – 7.8 mmol/L)
Cr – 63 mmol/L	(59 – 104 mmol/L)
CRP – 15 mg/L	(<5 mg/L)

Repeat PEFR – 34% of best

pH – 7.36	(7.35 – 7.45)
PaCO2 – 5.8 kPa	(4.7 – 6.0 kPa)
PaO2 – 9 kPa	(11 – 13 kPa)
HCO3 – 23 mEg/L	(22 – 26 mEg/L)

Answer: *The white blood cells are slightly raised and the CRP only slightly up, and so I think this is likely a picture of the inflammatory state rather than an acute infection: though the asthma exacerbation could be triggered by a viral infection. The U&Es are normal and the patient is not anaemic.*

The repeat PEFR is consistent with the first measurement, but there is the possibility of a slight trend down and so I would want to make sure this is repeated.

The arterial blood gas shows that the patient is hypoxic – this is a concern and is why I have given the patient oxygen. However, the pH and PaCO2 are normal which is more reassuring, but this gas warrants repeating following several rounds of treatment to ensure that the PaCO2 is not rising (and that the PaO2 is responding).

Interviewer: What would your next course of action be?

Answer: *I would continue with the back-to-back nebulisers, and continue down the BTS treatment pathway of an acute severe asthma attack. However, given all of the above, I am concerned about this patient's risk for further deterioration, and so would review with my senior and contact the intensive care team to make them aware of the patient at this early stage as it is clear that there is a significant potential for deterioration.*

Analysis: The candidate has talked through this scenario in an organised and professional manner. They are aware of the urgency of the situation, and have involved their seniors early as well as commencing immediate treatment with oxygen and nebulisers. They have identified the seriousness of the attack, and mentioned to the interviewers that they know where to look for further information (the British Thoracic Society guidelines). They also discuss appropriate investigation and further escalation as required.

Top Tip! British Thoracic Society Guidelines make for essential reading when revising the treatment of asthma. These can be found at:
https://www.brit-thoracic.org.uk

When revising these guidelines, ensure that you can identify the seriousness of the asthma attack based on the clinical criteria outlined in their guidelines. This is essential because it guides the treatment that you give, and determines when escalation to intensive care should be performed.

Scenario 12:

A 68 year old male patient presents to A&E with fresh red blood bleeding from the back passage. His observations on arrival are: HR 110, BP 90/60, Sats 98%, RR 18, Temp 37.1. You are the FY2 on-call for General Surgery and have been asked to clerk this patient.

Interviewer: How would you approach this scenario?

Answer: *My first course of action would be to perform a full A through E assessment of this patient, ensuring that his airway, breathing and circulation were intact. It sounds like this patient is haemodynamically unstable and so before continuing further, I would ensure I have wide-pore IV access in both antecubital fossae. I will take a full set of blood tests which will include an FBC, U&Es, CRP, LFTs, clotting profile, venous blood gas and group and save. I will start intravenous fluid resuscitation with 1 litre of crystalloid such as Hartman's solution. Once I have achieved an improvement in blood pressure and heart rate, I would then proceed to complete my A to E assessment. The patient will also require a urinary catheter to monitor urine output; since they are acutely bleeding, I would like to ensure that they are perfusing their kidneys. Urine output is a marker of end-organ function.*

I would then take a full history and examine this patient, which will include a PR examination with a chaperone present. I would elicit how long the patient had been bleeding, the type of blood: whether this was dark in colour suggesting an Upper GI source of bleeding such as a gastric ulcer or bright red in colour which is more indicative of a Lower GI source, how much blood they felt they had passed each time, whether it was only during bowel movements or in between as well, and assess for red flag symptoms such as weight loss and change in bowel habit.

Interviewer: What are some sources of Lower GI bleeding?

Answer: *There are a number of sources of Lower GI bleeding; these include diverticulae, haemorrhoids, fissures and tumours.*

Interviewer: The patient's haemoglobin is 65 and there is bright red blood on your glove when you examine the patient. What do you do next?

Answer: *This is suggestive of active bleeding, and according to guidelines, an Hb < 70 would be an indication for a blood transfusion. I would ensure this patient is cross-matched and inform my senior. It may be that if the patient is haemodynamically stable, he should undergo a CT angiogram to identify the bleeding point, and then with the help of interval radiology, it could be embolised to be controlled. However, if he is unstable then he will require further resuscitation with blood products. I would consider putting out a major haemorrhage protocol.*

Analysis: This is a thorough run-through of dealing with a patient presenting with an acute PR bleed. It is important to identify the differentials of PR bleeding, ranging from benign conditions such as diverticulae to malignancy. In suspected diverticular bleeds, CT imaging can help look for diverticulitis and identify if there is active bleeding to look for an embolisation point.

Scenario 13:

A 68 year old female patient with a background of COPD presents to A&E with increasing wheeze over the last few weeks, and with a slightly purulent cough that she hasn't been able to shake. Her observations on arrival are: HR 80, BP 137/93, Sats 89%, RR 26, Temp 37.9. You are the FY1 doctor and have been asked to clerk this patient.

Interviewer: How would you approach this scenario?

Answer: *My first course of action would be to perform a full A through E assessment of this patient, ensuring that her airway, breathing and circulation were intact. It sounds like this patient is wheezy and tachypnoeic, and so before further history and examination I would probably perform an ABG and commence salbutamol nebulisers in an attempt to improve her respiratory rate and determine how badly her acid-base balance has been affected.*

I would then take a full history and examine this patient with particular focus on the respiratory system. Amongst other items, I would want to determine if there is a formal diagnosis of COPD, and how many infections she has had over the last year. I would want to isolate if there were any obvious signs of consolidation or wheeze on exam. I would aim to maintain her oxygen saturations within the 88-92% range at this time unless I was concerned that she was becoming acutely hypoxic in which case I would escalate the oxygen therapy as required.

I would investigate with bloods (FBC, U&Es, LFTs, CRP, and clotting) and an arterial blood gas. I would monitor the temperature closely as there appears to be a low-grade pyrexia, but this wouldn't trigger criteria for blood cultures at this stage. I would however arrange for sputum culture to be sent and would also request that the patient's urinary legionella and pneumocystis antigens be tested. I would obtain a chest x-ray, looking for any obvious consolidation, and perhaps signs of chronic COPD changes (including hyperexpanded fields).

Interviewer: Here are some of the investigation results: what is your interpretation of them?

RESULTS:

Hb – 160 g/L	(115 – 165 g/L)
WCC – 14.3 x10⁹/L	(4 – 11 x10⁹/L)
Plt – 343 x10⁹/L	(150 – 450 x10⁹/L)
Na – 144 mmol/L	(133 – 146 mmol/L)
K – 5.0 mmol/L	(3.5 – 5.3 mmol/L)
Ur – 7.3 mmol/L	(2.5 – 7.8 mmol/L)
Cr – 110 mmol/L	(59 – 104 mmol/L)
ALT – 30 iU/L	(<33 iU/L)
ALP – 87 iU/L	(30 – 130 iU/L)
CRP – 98 mg/L	(<5 mg/L)
INR – 0.9	
pH – 7.32	(7.35 – 7.45)
PaCO2 – 6.6 kPa	(4.7 – 6.0 kPa)
PaO2 – 9.3 kPa	(11 – 13 kPa)
HCO3 – 27.3 mEg/L	(22 – 26 mEg/L)

Answer: *The white blood cells and CRP are raised: this makes me think there may be an underlying infection triggering this exacerbation of COPD.*

The U&Es suggest that the patient may be a little dry, and so I would commence fluid rehydration therapy.

I am somewhat concerned about the ABG: the patient demonstrates a partially compensated respiratory acidosis. I am concerned about the high PaCO2 as the patient may be entering type 2 respiratory failure.

Interviewer: What would your next course of action be?

Answer: *I would continue with salbutamol nebulisers, add ipratropium nebulisers and would consider commencing the patient on a course of 30mg prednisolone orally for 5 days.*

I feel that the patient likely has an infective cause to this presentation – given the cough, possible low-grade pyrexia, and investigation results – and so, in addition, I would like to start her on appropriate antibiotic therapy. At this stage this sounds like an infective exacerbation of COPD and so I would commence doxycycline, however if the chest x ray revealed an underlying pneumonia then I would treat with the appropriate antibiotic relative to her underlying CURB65 score.

I would want to try the patient with the initial therapy I mentioned, but if the PaCO2 does not improve on repeat ABG testing then this is an indication that the patient may require non-invasive ventilation, and so I would escalate the patient to my seniors, enquiring as to the possibility of a non-invasive ventilation bed either on a respiratory ward or medical high-dependency.

I would also ensure that I made a referral to the community outreach COPD team in hospital in an attempt to ensure the patient would be discharged in a timely fashion, should she improve with the above treatment.

Analysis: This is a thorough run-through of dealing with a patient presenting with what is likely an exacerbation of COPD. The candidate appropriately assessed the patient acutely, and commenced the correct treatment in this case. They demonstrated good investigative knowledge – not forgetting to request a sputum culture and urinary antigen testing. They also mentioned that they would refer to the community COPD team in hospital to try and facilitate patient discharge, an important thing to remember when part of the admitting team.

Top Tip! Ensure you are familiar with the different findings that can be present on an ABG as they are a common source of data interpretation in the interview.

Scenario 14:

An 82 year old male nursing home resident is brought to A&E as the nursing home staff noticed that he started coughing quite severely since lunch. His observations on arrival are: HR 64, BP 130/92, Sats 92%, RR 24, Temp 36.9. You are the FY1 doctor on call and have been asked to see this patient.

Interviewer: How would you approach this scenario?

Answer: *My immediate thought is that this patient may be suffering from an aspiration pneumonitis/pneumonia. This is due to his background of living in a nursing home and the fact that he started coughing following a meal. On arrival to the patient I would perform a full A through E assessment. The observations suggest to me that he may be a little hypoxic, and so I would commence oxygen therapy assuming he had no background of COPD.*

Once satisfied with the rest of the A to E assessment, I would then turn to performing a full history and thorough clinical examination. I would want to determine what exactly happened and if the patient can remember the events. I would want to know if he has known problems with his swallow, and this may require collateral history from the nursing home. If I felt he was likely to have an unsafe swallow (I could ask him to take a small sip of water to give me an idea) then I would make him nil by mouth and commence him on IV fluid supplementation.

I would determine whether there were any obvious signs on clinical examination of pneumonia or respiratory pathology. I would ensure bloods are sent (including FBC, U&Es, LFTs, and CRP). I would try to send a sample of his sputum for culture and perform urinary antigen testing. I would request an urgent chest x ray, as if the patient has aspirated then he may show signs of this in his right lower lobe.

Interviewer: Here are some of the investigation results: what is your interpretation of them?

RESULTS:

Hb – 125 g/L		*(130 – 180 g/L)*	
WCC – 10.3 x10⁹/L		*(4 – 11 x10⁹/L)*	
Plt – 159 x10⁹/L		*(150 – 450 x10⁹/L)*	

Hb – 125 g/L   *(130 – 180 g/L)*
WCC – 10.3 x10^9/L   *(4 – 11 x10^9/L)*
Plt – 159 x10^9/L   *(150 – 450 x10^9/L)*

Na – 139 mmol/L   *(133 – 146 mmol/L)*
K – 3.9 mmol/L   *(3.5 – 5.3 mmol/L)*
Ur – 7.1 mmol/L   *(2.5 – 7.8 mmol/L)*
Cr – 96 mmol/L   *(59 – 104 mmol/L)*

ALT – 27 iU/L   *(<33 iU/L)*
ALP – 54 iU/L   *(30 – 130 iU/L)*

CRP – 7 mg/L   *(<5 mg/L)*

Answer: *The patient is slightly anaemic, and so sending haematinics would be appropriate. His U&Es are within normal limits, though the urea is at the upper limit of normal, as is the creatinine, and so I would look to see if we had a baseline on the system and if not I would start slow IV fluid rehydration to try to reduce the risk of the patient developing an AKI. The patient's inflammatory markers are essentially within normal limits, and this would fit with an acute presentation of a possible aspiration pneumonitis.*

Interviewer: What would your next course of action be?

Answer: *I would continue with supportive management, and would await the chest x ray. I would review the case with my registrar. If the patient was not improving within 24-48 hours then I would consider further management with empirical antibiotics such as levofloxacin, and potential further investigations such as CT imaging or bronchoalveolar lavage after discussion with a senior.*

Analysis: The candidate correctly makes the initial diagnosis but does so in a way that shows that they realise the initial presentation in cases such as this is with aspiration pneumonitis as opposed to aspiration pneumonia – which potentially can develop later. Therefore, they correctly assess and treat the patient in the acute situation, and they also avoid inappropriate antibiotic therapy. They clarify this, however, with knowledge of what they would do should the patient not be improving.

Top Tip! Aspiration pneumonitis is a common presentation from nursing homes. The aspirate is often aspirated down the right main bronchus (due to it being a more "vertical" route into the lungs), and so that is frequently where chest x ray changes are seen. It is also important to remember that these patients usually don't require antibiotic therapy initially – at this acute stage there is likely no infection present, and so simply providing supportive care as required is the treatment. If the patient starts to deteriorate (usually 24-48 hours later), then this is when you should consider repeat investigation and possible antibiotic therapy. Local policy documents differ on when and what antibiotic to prescribe, and so it is always important to check there first.

Scenario 15:

A 53 year old obese male patient has been admitted with adhesional small bowel obstruction and is undergoing conservative treatment with an NG tube and IV fluids. He has been on the surgical ward for 4 days but is not showing signs of improvement; he is yet to pass any flatus. His HR is 125, his BP is 75/40, Sats 97% on 2L oxygen, RR 25 and Temp 37.5. You are the FY1 on-call for General Surgery and have been asked to assess this patient as he is becoming increasingly short of breath and has developed a productive cough.

Interviewer: How would you approach this scenario?

Answer: *The first thing I would do on arrival to this patient is to perform a full ABCDE assessment and ensure that he is clinically stable. I will ensure he has wide-bore IV access. He will require IV fluid resuscitation using crystalloids such as Hartman's. I will take a full set of blood tests which will include an FBC, U&Es, CRP, blood cultures and an arterial blood gas to look at pH, pCO_2, pO_2 and lactate. I will perform a cardiovascular and respiratory system examination, in particular auscultate his chest.*

I would take a full history to elicit the nature of his shortness of breath and cough. Initial investigations would include a 12-lead ECG and a chest x-ray to look for signs of ischaemia to look for any evidence of acute coronary syndrome, and nya consolidation which may suggest a hospital-acquired pneumonia or aspiration pneumonia.

Interviewer: His chest x-ray shows a dense right middle zone consolidation, he has right lower zone crackles, and he has deranged inflammatory markers. What will you do next?

Answer: *These findings are suggestive of a hospital-acquired pneumonia. I will commence IV antibiotics as per trust guidelines. I will repeat my ABCDE assessment and check if he has responded to IV fluid resuscitation. If not, I will consider inserting a urinary catheter to monitor urine output. I will inform my seniors of my management plan and request a senior review.*

Analysis: Patients who have prolonged hospital admissions are at risk of hospital-acquired pneumonia (HAP), especially if they do not mobilise, are elderly and have underlying respiratory conditions such as COPD. Although this is case is not the new presentation of an acute surgical pathology, it is a common complication that surgical inpatients may experience. In this case, it is important to perform a thorough assessment of the patient, request appropriate investigations and commence initial treatment. It is also important to re-assess them from a surgical perspective to see if their admitting pathology has not progressed further as this may require urgent surgical intervention; hence the importance of early senior involvement.

Discussions with other specialities such as General Medicine and Intensive Care for advice or a review should be well-prepared for; have all the relevant investigations and results to hand such as latest blood tests, blood gas readings and radiology findings. Try to anticipate what questions your medical or intensivist colleague may ask. Use the 'SBAR' structure as this will help guide your discussion and will ensure you do not miss any important details. Remember, the person on the other end of the line is likely to be as busy, if not busier than you are.

Scenario 16:

A 53 year old male patient has been admitted with a pneumonia and is on the respiratory ward. He reports to the nursing staff that he has developed severe crushing central chest pain. His HR is 74, his BP is 153/90, Sats 97%, RR 18 and Temp 37. You are the FY1 doctor on call and have been asked to assess this patient.

Interviewer: How would you approach this scenario?

Answer: *The first thing I would do on arrival to this patient is to perform a full ABCDE assessment and ensure that he is clinically stable. If he was still in chest pain I would ensure that an ECG is performed urgently, as well as providing initial treatment for ACS as my suspicions are high: I would provide oxygen, morphine, 300mg Aspirin and a GTN spray.*

If there were ST elevation changes on the ECG then I would contact my senior and my local PCI centre urgently, and see whether I could arrange transfer for treatment.

Following this, I would continue my full history and examination: I would want to ensure I identified exactly when the pain began, the character of the pain, if he has had it before, if he has any cardiac history, as well as completing my full systems review and background social and family history. I would perform a full cardiology examination, looking for any heart murmurs or signs of cardiac decompensation.

I would then begin investigating the cause for the patient's presentation. I mentioned the ECG earlier, and would have this repeated urgently if there were any further episodes of chest pain. It would be important to perform an initial set of bloods, including FBC, U&Es, clotting and also a troponin. I would then need to correlate this result with a 6-hour troponin to observe if there were any dynamic changes. I would also perform a chest x-ray.

Interviewer: Here are some of the investigation results: what is your interpretation of them?

RESULTS:

Hb – 143 g/L	*(130 – 180 g/L)*
WCC – 10.9 x10⁹/L	*(4 – 11 x10⁹/L)*
Plt – 402 x10⁹/L	*(150 – 450 x10⁹/L)*
Na – 142 mmol/L	*(133 – 146 mmol/L)*
K – 4.9 mmol/L	*(3.5 – 5.3 mmol/L)*
Ur – 4.8 mmol/L	*(2.5 – 7.8 mmol/L)*
Cr – 73 mmol/L	*(59 – 104 mmol/L)*
INR 1.0	
Troponin T – 25 ng/L	*(<14 ng/L)*
Repeat Troponin T – 281 ng/L	*(<14 ng/L)*

Answer: *The FBC and U&Es are normal with the exception of the slightly raised white blood cells: though this could be explained by the fact that the patient was admitted with pneumonia. The patient's troponin has shown a significant rise at the second measurement, and this confirms the fact that he has indeed had an acute coronary episode.*

Interviewer: What would your next course of action be?
Answer: *Given the fact that I have confirmed ACS in this patient I would ensure that I have discussed this patient with my senior if this had not already been done. As per guidelines, I would prescribe fondaparinux. If the ECG showed ST elevation then I would call my local PCI centre to try to arrange transfer, and if the ECG did not show signs of ST elevation I would arrange for transfer to a Coronary Care Unit.*

The patient should also have secondary prevention medication prescribed: these would include dual antiplatelet therapy, a statin, a beta-blocker and an angiotensin converting enzyme inhibitor (ACEi).

As mentioned, I would discuss this case with my senior to make sure they were happy with the management plan that I have initiated, and to check if if they felt the patient needed to be moved to the Coronary Care Unit.

Analysis: Once again, the candidate performs a successful initial assessment of the patient. They manage the patient appropriately, and identify that the patient may need transfer for PCI therapy if certain criteria are met. They correctly investigate the cause for the patient's presentation, and take an appropriate history and examination. The discuss early and often with their senior. Finally, the candidate correctly identifies the required secondary prevention.

Top Tip! Acute Coronary Syndrome is a common interview topic, and the treatment for this should flow off the tip of your tongue. Be sure to revise ECGs, as the interviewers may show you an ECG with an infarct present, and may ask you to identify the abnormality, including where it is anatomically located.

Scenario 17:

You are the FY1 doctor on call for the wards in a District General Hospital. A 37 year old male patient was admitted two days ago following his first ever seizure with no apparent cause found, and is being prepared for discharge. However, the nurse calls you overnight informing you that the patient has become quite confused, aggressive, and is seeing objects that aren't there. She says he looks hot and sweaty, but doesn't have recent observations.

Interviewer: How would you approach this scenario?

Answer: *I am concerned in this case that the patient may be withdrawing from alcohol, and possible may have developed Delirium Tremens. This is an emergency and so I would attend the patient as soon as possible. Indeed, the withdrawal may have been the initial reason for his presentation with a seizure. I would ask the nurse on the phone that, if she felt the situation was safe enough, she should perform a full set of observations and I would be there as soon as possible.*

On arrival I would perform a full A through E assessment of the patient. I would then try to engage with him in conversation and determine how unwell he actually was at this moment in time. I would look through the observations and commence further investigation, whilst trying to obtain a quick alcohol consumption history from the patient if he were able to provide this.

I would investigate the patient by performing an ECG and a capillary blood glucose reading. I would send a full set of bloods, including FBC, U&Es, LFTs, CRP, Bone Profile, magnesium, glucose, amylase and a clotting screen. I would perform an arterial blood gas looking for signs of metabolic acidosis. I would review the requirement for CT imaging of the patient's head depending on if any imaging has been performed since arrival and if the patient has had any trauma to his head since being in hospital.

Interviewer: Here are some of the investigation results: what is your interpretation of them?

RESULTS:

Hb – 137 g/L	(130 – 180 g/L)
WCC – 5.2 x10^9/L	(4 – 11 x10^9/L)
Plt – 158 x10^9/L	(150 – 450 x10^9/L)
Na – 135 mmol/L	(133 – 146 mmol/L)
K – 3.6 mmol/L	(3.5 – 5.3 mmol/L)
Ur – 2.6 mmol/L	(2.5 – 7.8 mmol/L)
Cr – 73 mmol/L	(59 – 104 mmol/L)
Corrected Ca – 2.3 mmol/L	(2.2 – 2.6 mmol/L)
PO4 – 0.9 mmol/L	(0.8 – 1.4 mmol/L)
Magnesium – 0.8 mmol/L	(0.7 – 1.0 mmol/L)
ALT – 46 iU/L	(<33 iU/L)
ALP – 65 iU/L	(30 – 130 iU/L)
CRP – <5 mg/L	(<5 mg/L)
Amylase – 43 iU/dL	(28 –100 iU/dL)
Serum Glucose – 7 mmol/L	(<7.8 mmol/L
INR – 1.1	

Answer: *Most of the blood tests given here are normal. The patient's ALT is slightly raised, which could fit with a picture of liver-disease. However, and reassuringly from a possible seizure point of view, the Magnesium, Calcium, Phosphate and glucose are normal, along with the other electrolytes. The bloods also serve to reduce the likelihood of other potential causes of delirium such as infection and electrolyte disturbances.*

Interviewer: What would your next course of action be?

Answer: *I would review this case with my senior, and I would ask about commencing treatment for alcohol withdrawal: I would follow my local Trust's protocol in prescribing benzodiazepines for the patient (usually chlordiazepoxide) as well as prescribing high-dose pabrinex. I let my senior know that I may need to escalate this patient further if he did not respond to the above therapy.*

Analysis: The candidate has a good patient-centred approach, and identifies that they need more information about the patient's observations but only as long as this wouldn't affect the safety of staff on the ward. They correctly identify the key to the scenario, which is that it is likely that the patient has had a diagnosis of alcohol withdrawal missed. The candidate also identifies that the patient is acutely and severely unwell, and that they need urgent medical attention. They candidate investigates the patient in an effective and thorough manner, and initiates the appropriate therapy in cases of alcohol withdrawal. They also explain that they would contact their senior, which is very appropriate in this case due to the potential severity of Delirium Tremens.

> ***Top Tip!*** Acute alcohol withdrawal and decompensated liver disease are other common cases that come up in interviews and so it is important to be familiar with the diagnosis and management of these conditions.

Further Example Scenarios

We now cover some additional scenarios that may come up during the interview. We do not provide full sample answers, but rather the questions as they may be asked in the interview (following the format used above), and example investigation results. The idea is that you may wish to work through these scenarios with a friend who is also preparing for the AFP interviews. There is an answer page detailing the main aspects to include in each of these scenarios at the end.

Additional Scenario 1:

A 35 year old male patient presents to the A&E department with a history of weight loss, tiredness, and very severe diarrhoea for the last several days. He attends with his male partner. His HR is 87, his BP is 118/70, Sats 98%, RR 18 and Temp 37.8. You are the FY1 doctor on call and have been asked to clerk this patient.

Interviewer: How would you approach this scenario?

Interviewer: Here are some of the investigation results: what is your interpretation of them?

RESULTS:

Hb – 119 g/L	(130 – 180 g/L)
WCC – 3.4 x10⁹/L	(4 – 11 x10⁹/L)
Lymphocytes – 0.3 x10⁹/L	(1 - 3 x10⁹/L)
Neutrophils – 3.0 x10⁹/L	(2 - 7 x10⁹/L)
Plt – 172 x10⁹/L	(150 – 450 x10⁹/L)
Na – 141 mmol/L	(133 – 146 mmol/L)
K – 4.1 mmol/L	(3.5 – 5.3 mmol/L)
Ur – 8.9 mmol/L	(2.5 – 7.8 mmol/L)
Cr – 131 mmol/L	(59 – 104 mmol/L)
CRP – 84 mg/L	(<5 mg/L)

Interviewer: What would your next course of action be?
Additional Scenario 2:

You are the FY1 doctor in A&E. You are asked to clerk a 21 year old male patient who presents with vomiting and severe abdominal pain. His observations on arrival are: HR is 98, his BP is 112/68, Sats 97%, RR 20 and Temp 37. His partner reports that he has become increasingly drowsy since arriving in the department.

Interviewer: How would you approach this scenario?

Interviewer: Here are some of the investigation results: what is your interpretation of them?

Interviewer: What would your next course of action be?

RESULTS:

Hb – 117 g/L	(130 – 180 g/L)
WCC – 12.1 x10⁹/L	(4 – 11 x10⁹/L)
Plt – 291 x10⁹/L	(150 – 450 x10⁹/L)
Na – 143 mmol/L	(133 – 146 mmol/L)
K – 5.2 mmol/L	(3.5 – 5.3 mmol/L)
Ur – 6.9 mmol/L	(2.5 – 7.8 mmol/L)
Cr – 101 mmol/L	(59 – 104 mmol/L)
CRP – <5 mg/L	(<5 mg/L)
INR – 1.0	
Glucose – 21 mmol/L	(<7 mmol/L)
pH – 7.29	(7.35 – 7.45)
PaCO2 – 5.2 kPa	(4.7 – 6.0 kPa)
PaO2 – 12.3 kPa	(11 – 13 kPa)
HCO3 – 18 mEg/L	(22 – 26 mEg/L)

Urinalysis:
Protein – +
Blood – Negative
Glucose – ++
Ketones – +++

Additional Scenario 3:

A 25 year old woman presents to the MAU with nausea, vomiting and abdominal pain with occasional diarrhoea for the last three days. She denies any other symptoms of note. Her HR is 73, her BP is 120/83, Sats 97%, RR 16 and Temp 36.9. You, as the FY1 on call, have been asked to review her.

Interviewer: How would you approach this scenario?

Interviewer: Here are some of the investigation results: what is your interpretation of them?

RESULTS:

Hb – 132 g/L	*(115 – 165 g/L)*
WCC – 14.9 x10⁹/L	*(4 – 11 x10⁹/L)*
Plt – 239 x10⁹/L	*(150 – 450 x10⁹/L)*
Na – 140 mmol/L	*(133 – 146 mmol/L)*
K – 3.9 mmol/L	*(3.5 – 5.3 mmol/L)*
Ur – 7.9 mmol/L	*(2.5 – 7.8 mmol/L)*
Cr – 92 mmol/L	*(59 – 104 mmol/L)*
CRP – 59 mg/L	*(<5 mg/L)*

Interviewer: What would your next course of action be?

Additional Scenario 4:

A 57 year old lady presents to the Medical Assessment Unit with left leg erythema and swelling. You have been asked to clerk her in and arrange for investigation as required. Her HR is 82, her BP is 133/94, Sats 97%, RR 18 and Temp 37.

Interviewer: How would you approach this scenario?

Interviewer: Here are some of the investigation results: what is your interpretation of them?

RESULTS:

Hb – 127 g/L	*(115 – 165 g/L)*
WCC – 7.4 x10⁹/L	*(4 – 11 x10⁹/L)*
Plt – 360 x10⁹/L	*(150 – 450 x10⁹/L)*
Na – 140 mmol/L	*(133 – 146 mmol/L)*
K – 4.7 mmol/L	*(3.5 – 5.3 mmol/L)*
Ur – 3.9 mmol/L	*(2.5 – 7.8 mmol/L)*
Cr – 64 mmol/L	*(59 – 104 mmol/L)*
CRP – <5 mg/L	*(<5 mg/L)*
INR – 1.1	
D-Dimer 280 ng/ml	*(<230 ng/ml)*

Interviewer: What would your next course of action be?

Additional Scenario 5:

A 34 year old intravenous drug user presents with recurrent fevers and shortness of breath. On examination it has been reported that the patient has evidence of splinter haemorrhages and a murmur. His HR is 88, his BP is 123/78, Sats 95%, RR 17 and Temp 37.9. You are the FY1 doctor on call and have been asked to assess the patient.

Interviewer: How would you approach this scenario?

Interviewer: Here are some of the investigation results: what is your interpretation of them?

RESULTS:

Hb – 123 g/L	(130 – 180 g/L)
WCC – 11.9 x10⁹/L	(4 – 11 x10⁹/L)
Plt – 181 x10⁹/L	(150 – 450 x10⁹/L)
Na – 135 mmol/L	(133 – 146 mmol/L)
K – 3.8 mmol/L	(3.5 – 5.3 mmol/L)
Ur – 5.8 mmol/L	(2.5 – 7.8 mmol/L)
Cr – 73 mmol/L	(59 – 104 mmol/L)
CRP – 124 mg/L	(<5 mg/L)
INR – 0.9	

Interviewer: What would your next course of action be?

Additional Scenario 6:

You are the FY1 doctor or call and have been asked to clerk a 35 year old woman who presents with acute shortness of breath and pleuritic chest pain. She denies any past medical history, with the exception of 3 miscarriages. Her HR is 82, her BP is 123/84, Sats 94%, RR 22 and Temp 36.8.

Interviewer: How would you approach this scenario?

Interviewer: Here are some of the investigation results: what is your interpretation of them?

RESULTS:

Hb – 132 g/L	(115 – 165 g/L)
WCC – 4.9 x10⁹/L	(4 – 11 x10⁹/L)
Plt – 369 x10⁹/L	(150 – 450 x10⁹/L)
Na – 137 mmol/L	(133 – 146 mmol/L)
K – 4.7 mmol/L	(3.5 – 5.3 mmol/L)
Ur – 4.2 mmol/L	(2.5 – 7.8 mmol/L)
Cr – 80 mmol/L	(59 – 104 mmol/L)
CRP – 14 mg/L	(<5 mg/L)
INR – 1.0	
Oxygen saturations – 91%	(94 – 98 %)
D-Dimer 280 ng/ml	(<230 ng/ml)

Interviewer: What would your next course of action be?

Additional Scenario 7:

A 28 year old woman has returned from travelling in Africa, and presents with headache, fever and shortness of breath. Her HR is 94, her BP is 109/65, Sats 97%, RR 19 and Temp 38.5. You are a member of the acute medical team, and have been asked to clerk this patient.

Interviewer: How would you approach this scenario?

Interviewer: Here are some of the investigation results: what is your interpretation of them?

RESULTS:

Hb – 107 g/L   (115 – 165 g/L)
WCC – 12.4 x10⁹/L   (4 – 11 x10⁹/L)
Plt – 190 x10⁹/L   (150 – 450 x10⁹/L)

Na – 139 mmol/L   (133 – 146 mmol/L)
K – 4.9 mmol/L   (3.5 – 5.3 mmol/L)
Ur – 3.2 mmol/L   (2.5 – 7.8 mmol/L)
Cr – 73 mmol/L   (59 – 104 mmol/L)

CRP – 63 mg/L   (<5 mg/L)

Interviewer: What would your next course of action be?

Additional Scenario 8:

A 53 year old gentleman presents with an acutely red, painful and swollen right first metatarsophalangeal joint. His HR is 68, his BP is 148/91, Sats 97%, RR 18 and Temp 37. You have been asked to assess this patient.

Interviewer: How would you approach this scenario?

Interviewer: Here are some of the investigation results: what is your interpretation of them?

RESULTS:

Hb – 167 g/L	(130 – 180 g/L)
WCC – 5.8 x10⁹/L	(4 – 11 x10⁹/L)
Plt – 228 x10⁹/L	(150 – 450 x10⁹/L)
Na – 139 mmol/L	(133 – 146 mmol/L)
K – 4.1 mmol/L	(3.5 – 5.3 mmol/L)
Ur – 4.5 mmol/L	(2.5 – 7.8 mmol/L)
Cr –73 mmol/L	(59 – 104 mmol/L)
CRP – 28 mg/L	(<5 mg/L)
INR – 1.0	

Interviewer: What would your next course of action be?

Additional Scenario 9:

An 82 year old female patient presents with a rash on her left lower limb, which started 4 days ago and has become hot and swollen. There is a small ulcer on the medial aspect of the area. Her HR is 85, her BP is 118/68, Sats 97%, RR 18 and Temp 38.1. You have been asked to see this patient in MAU.

Interviewer: How would you approach this scenario?

Interviewer: Here are some of the investigation results: what is your interpretation of them?

RESULTS:

Hb – 113 g/L	(115 – 165 g/L)
WCC – 15.2 x10⁹/L	(4 – 11 x10⁹/L)
Plt – 231 x10⁹/L	(150 – 450 x10⁹/L)
Na – 135 mmol/L	(133 – 146 mmol/L)
K – 4.5 mmol/L	(3.5 – 5.3 mmol/L)
Ur – 9.3 mmol/L	(2.5 – 7.8 mmol/L)
Cr – 109 mmol/L	(59 – 104 mmol/L)
CRP – 83 mg/L	(<5 mg/L)

Interviewer: What would your next course of action be?

Additional Scenario 10:

You are the FY1 doctor on call and have been asked to clerk a 71 year old male in MAU. He presents with a 6 week history of weight loss, night sweats and intermittent fever. He has lost his appetite, and feels his strength is waning. There is mild left inguinal lymphadenopathy, and you note what you think is a large spleen. His HR is 66, his BP is 132/90, Sats 98%, RR 18 and Temp 37.

Interviewer: How would you approach this scenario?

Interviewer: Here are some of the investigation results: what is your interpretation of them?

RESULTS:

Hb – 120 g/L	(130 – 180 g/L)
WCC – 59 x10⁹/L	(4 – 11 x10⁹/L)
Plt – 159 x10⁹/L	(150 – 450 x10⁹/L)
Na – 137 mmol/L	(133 – 146 mmol/L)
K – 4.8 mmol/L	(3.5 – 5.3 mmol/L)
Ur – 5.9 mmol/L	(2.5 – 7.8 mmol/L)
Cr – 82 mmol/L	(59 – 104 mmol/L)
Corrected Ca – 2.7 mmol/L	(2.2 – 2.6 mmol/L)
CRP – <5 mg/L	(<5 mg/L)

Interviewer: What would your next course of action be?

Additional Scenario 11:

A 59 year old male smoker presents with haemoptysis for the past 7 days. This has never happened before and he is very concerned. His HR is 88, his BP is 138/89, Sats 96%, RR 20 and Temp 37. You, as part of the on call team, have been asked to review the patient.

Interviewer: How would you approach this scenario?

Interviewer: Here are some of the investigation results: what is your interpretation of them?

RESULTS:

Hb – 140 g/L	*(130 – 180 g/L)*
WCC – 5.8 x10⁹/L	*(4 – 11 x10⁹/L)*
Plt – 237 x10⁹/L	*(150 – 450 x10⁹/L)*
Na – 139 mmol/L	*(133 – 146 mmol/L)*
K – 4.5 mmol/L	*(3.5 – 5.3 mmol/L)*
Ur – 6.2 mmol/L	*(2.5 – 7.8 mmol/L)*
Cr – 78 mmol/L	*(59 – 104 mmol/L)*
CRP – <5 mg/L	*(<5 mg/L)*

Interviewer: What would your next course of action be?

Additional Scenario 12:

A 74 year old male patient presents with increasing shortness of breath and some weight gain over the last 2 months. He thinks that his ankles are more swollen than they used to be. He reports that his exercise tolerance has reduced significantly, and that he occasionally feels as if his chest is very tight, but denies palpitations and chest pain. His HR is 74, his BP is 151/94, Sats 96%, RR 22 and Temp 37. You are the FY1 doctor on call and have been asked to clerk this patient in MAU.

Interviewer: How would you approach this scenario?

Interviewer: Here are some of the investigation results: what is your interpretation of them?

RESULTS:

Hb – 129 g/L	(130 – 180 g/L)
WCC – 6.7 x10⁹/L	(4 – 11 x10⁹/L)
Plt – 209 x10⁹/L	(150 – 450 x10⁹/L)
Na – 142 mmol/L	(133 – 146 mmol/L)
K – 3.8 mmol/L	(3.5 – 5.3 mmol/L)
Ur – 6.1 mmol/L	(2.5 – 7.8 mmol/L)
Cr – 94 mmol/L	(59 – 104 mmol/L)
CRP – 3 mg/L	(<5 mg/L)
BNP – 381 pg/ml	(<100 pg/ml)

Interviewer: What would your next course of action be?

Additional Scenario 13:

A 60 year old male patient presents to the A&E department with back pain, and urinary and faecal incontinence which has been present for the last 2 days. He describes 'shooting pains' going down his legs.

Interviewer: What are your main differentials?

Interviewer: What investigations will you request?

Interviewer: What would your next course of action be?

Additional Scenario 14:

You are the FY2 on-call for General Surgery. You are asked to clerk a 61 year old male patient who presents with vomiting and severe abdominal pain, distension and absolute constipation.

Interviewer: How would you approach this scenario?

Interviewer: He has an abdominal x-ray which shows dilated loops of bowel in the centre of the film, what are your differentials?

Interviewer: What would your next course of action be?

Additional Scenario 15:

A 54 year old man is brought to the emergency department with severe central abdominal pain radiating to the back, he is pale, hypotensive and has reduced GCS. On examination, there is a large pulsatile mass in the central of his abdomen. The emergency department doctors have performed a 'point-of-care' ultrasound scan at the bedside which suggests a large abdominal aortic aneurysm with free fluid in the abdomen.

Interviewer: How would you approach this scenario?

Interviewer: He is known to be on the abdominal aortic aneurysm screening programme, how would you proceed?

Interviewer: What would your next course of action be?

Additional Scenario 16:

You are the FY2 on-call for Surgery have been asked to review a 69 year old lady who has presented with a cold, pulseless, pale leg. She is a smoker with a 20 pack-year history, and a 12 lead- ECG shows atrial fibrillation. She is otherwise stable but is in considerable amounts of pain.

Interviewer: What are your differentials?

Interviewer: How would you manage this patient?

Interviewer: What are some risk factors for peripheral vascular disease?

Additional Scenario 17:

You are a FY1 in General Surgery and have been asked to assess a 61 year old man on the ward who is 2 days post laparoscopic-assisted right hemicolectomy for colon cancer. He is complaining of increased abdominal pain, is febrile at 38.6°C and has gone into atrial fibrillation at 110bpm.

Interviewer: How would you approach this scenario?

Interviewer: What are your differentials? What investigations will you request?

Interviewer: You speak to your registrar who advises an urgent CT scan of the abdomen and pelvis. This confirms your suspicion of an anastomotic leak. What would your next course of action be?

Additional Scenario 18:

A 70 year old male is on the orthopaedic ward 4 days post fixation of an extracapsular neck of femur fracture. His main issue has been pain. You are asked to see him as he has become acutely hypoxic, short of breath with chest tightness.

Interviewer: How would you manage this patient?

Interviewer: What are your differentials? What do you think is the most likely?

Interviewer: What imaging would you request? What investigation would you requested for a suspected pulmonary embolism?

Interviewer: How would you treat this patient?

Example Scenarios: Answer Key

We provide here an answer key for the above Additional Scenarios. This ensures that you were on the correct path with your answers, and also illustrates some of the key points to make sure you cover if you are faced with any of these scenarios during the interview.

Additional Scenario 1:
Consider causes of immunosuppression

If considering Human Immunodeficiency Virus, think about diagnosis and think about ethical issues with contact tracing and confidentiality

Consider the likely organism in the presentation of Acquired Immunodeficiency Syndrome (AIDS)

Don't forget the likely AKI (consider all results given)

Additional Scenario 2:
Diabetic Ketoacidosis

Provide an explanation for all the results and how they contribute to your diagnosis

Don't forget aggressive fluid rehydration as part of the treatment plan

Follow local Trust's policy (see your intranet) on treatment with insulin

Additional Scenario 3:
Likely gastroenteritis

Consider potential causes, including viral

May be prudent to send stool culture

Don't forget all the bloods: the patient's Urea & Electrolytes suggest she may be dehydrated

Additional Scenario 4:
Deep vein thrombosis as probable diagnosis – don't forget to calculate the Well's score prior to D-dimer

Will require ultrasound Doppler

Patient will require treatment with anticoagulation if you cannot arrange the Doppler scan on the same day

Importance of exercise and raising leg to assist drainage

Additional Scenario 5:

Possible infective endocarditis

Consider different organisms and valves in intravenous drug users

Know what your local empirical antibiotic choices would be

Don't forget the 3 sets of cultures prior to antibiotic delivery

Needs urgent echocardiography along with urgent cardiology review

Additional Scenario 6:

Consider pulmonary embolism

Again, perform Well's score

Consider age of patient: will require preganancy test before further investigation

Consider recurrent miscarriages as possible clue to potential unifying diagnosis (anti-phospholipid syndrome)

Additional Scenario 7:

Fever in returning traveller could be due to a number of causes, but important to consider malaria here

Look at local policy: patient may require isolating

Ask about anti-malarial prophylaxis

Further investigation required includes blood film and cultures

Referral to local infectious diseases unit

Additional Scenario 8:

Have to rule out infected joint: septic arthritis is a medical emergency

Additional tests: blood uric acid levels and ESR, x ray, and potentially joint aspiration if effusion present

Consider treatment options, including colchicine and NSAIDs

Referral to orthopaedics and rheumatology as required

Additional Scenario 9:

Likely cellulitis

Ensure patient not septic: ABCDE approach

Swab ulcer for microbiology, be clinically of low risk of osteomyelitis or investigate further

Empirical antibiotics (flucloxacillin)

Don't forget all the bloods, patient's Urea & Electrolytes suggest she may have an AKI

Additional Scenario 10:

Haematological malignancy: need breakdown of white blood cell count to confirm diagnosis

Blood film required

Ultrasound abdomen to confirm splenomegaly

Haematology referral for likely bone marrow biopsy

Treatment of hypercalcaemia

Additional Scenario 11:

Urgent chest x ray required

Lung cancer until proven otherwise

Consider other differential diagnoses including tuberculosis, pneumonia and pulmonary embolism

May have communication skills discussion about breaking bad news to the patient

Additional Scenario 12:

May be the first presentation of heart failure

Requires chest x ray and echocardiogram

If fluid overload significant, then consider use of diuretics, but be careful of further derangements in urea and electrolytes

Additional Scenario 13:

Cauda equina syndrome.

This patient will require an urgent MRI scan of the spine to visualise his spinal cord and look for evidence of compression.

If positive, he will require urgent spinal decompression in theatre.

Do not forget to perform a thorough neurological assessment of this patients, examine dermatomes and myotomes, as well as perform a digital rectal examination as part of your assessment.

Additional Scenario 14:

Small bowel obstruction.

This patient will require management using the 'drip and suck' method; a nasogastric tube used to decompress the stomach of gastric contents; start with aspirating to dryness and leave the tube on free drainage, and then perform regular aspirates depending on output. Ensure the patient is on IV fluids initially for resuscitation purposes and then to support their renal function.

They will often require a CT scan of the abdomen and pelvis to identify the cause and look for a transition point in the bowel.

Additional Scenario 15:
Ruptured abdominal aortic aneurysm (AAA).

This is a very important differential that should be considered in almost all patients presenting with abdominal pain, particularly if it is central, radiating to the back or loin pain.

Know the principles of initial management, escalating early to seniors, and knowing when a patient is stable enough to be transferred for CT imaging to confirm rupture. Know the AAA screening programme guidelines. When are patients first invited? What are the management steps for the various diameter aneurysms?

Additional Scenario 16:
Acutely ischaemic limb likely secondary to an embolus in a patient with AF. Acute-on-chronic-thrombosis is also an important differential to consider.

Make sure you are aware of the 6 P's of peripheral vascular disease (painful, pale, pulseless, paraesthesiae, perishingly cold, paralysis).

Ankle-Brachial Pressure Index; how to determine this and what the values correspond to in terms of likely symtoms.

Investigations: Angiography (both percutaneous and CT), Duplex/Doppler, ABPI. Interventions: Angioplasty, bypass, amputation.

Additional Scenario 17:
Anastomotic leak.

Adequate resuscitation of the patient with appropriate investigations such as blood tests, blood cultures and urgent CT scan of the abdomen and pelvis to assess the anastomosis. Commence IV broad-spectrum antibiotics and insert a urinary catheter.

Awareness that lower anastomoses are at higher risk of leak to due to poorer blood supply. Other risk factors of anastomotic leak include smoking, diabetes, poor nutrition and immunosuppression.

Escalation to seniors. The patient may well need to return to theatre for a laparotomy and assessment of the anastomosis depending on a number of factors as well as CT findings.

Additional Scenario 18:

Pulmonary embolism.

Management would follow an ABCDE approach with ALS protocols. A full set of bloods including FBC, U&Es, CRP, and an arterial blood gas should be taken.

Investigations include a 12 lead ECG, chest x-ray, and CT pulmonary angiogram as the gold standard for a pulmonary embolism. You may also consider putting the patient on heart monitoring.

Treatment would normally be subcutaneous low molecular weight heparin at treatment dose, (note that you should check the drug chart to see if appropriate VTE prophylaxis has been given or not during this patient's admission, as well as co-morbidities and past medical history to look for previous VTE).

A haemodynamically unstable patient may be eligible for thrombolysis using a tissue plasminogen activator such as alteplase, after discussing with your own seniors and others such as the Medical SpR on-call and ICU SpR on-call.

ETHICAL SCENARIOS

As mentioned, it is quite possible for the interview to feature a discussion of an ethical scenario (or for specific ethical components of the clinical scenario to be discussed). This may focus on discussions regarding what to do in common clinical situations, or may cover a 'professionalism' scenario (dealing with difficult colleagues, for example). These situations can be closely intertwined. We will discuss the ethical scenario first.

The **ethical scenario** may involve a complex discussion regarding the capacity of a patient to make a treatment decision. It may discuss difficulties in deciding what to do in patients with mental health illnesses. The way to answer the scenario effectively is to ensure that you follow the underlying principles of Medical Ethics, and that you ensure that you always have the best interests of the patient at the centre of your argument.

The second component of this station is the **professionalism scenario**. This is designed to test your professional behaviour when put under a variety of different stressors (for example, what to do when there is a sick patient but you need to leave work for a social engagement).

We will first discuss some of the fundamental principles of medical ethics. We will then turn to sample scenarios and questions that may come up during the ethics scenario. Finally, we turn to a discussion of the professionalism issues and scenarios that may come up.

Medical Ethics

Most of you will be familiar with the core principles of medical ethics, having received teaching on this during medical school. If you desire a more formal refresher, then we would recommend reading *Medical Ethics: A Very Short Introduction* by Tony Hope, which gives a brief and accessible overview.

When presented with a question on medical ethics, it is essential to think about how the main principles of medical ethics apply.

The main principles of medical ethics are:

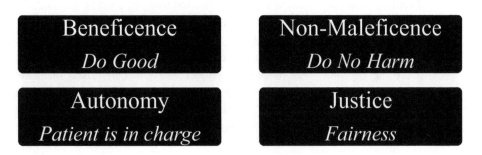

Beneficence	Non-Maleficence
Do Good	*Do No Harm*
Autonomy	Justice
Patient is in charge	*Fairness*

Beneficence

The wellbeing of the patient should be the doctor's first priority. In medicine, this means that one must act in the patient's best interests to ensure the best outcome is achieved for them, i.e. 'Do Good'.

Non-Maleficence

This is the principle of avoiding harm to the patient, keeping with the Hippocratic Oath "First do no harm". There can be a danger that in a willingness to treat, doctors can sometimes cause more harm to the patient than good. This can especially be the case with major interventions, such as chemotherapy or surgery. Where a course of action has both potential harms and potential benefits, non-maleficence must be balanced against beneficence.

Autonomy

The patient has the right to determine their own health care. This, therefore, requires the doctor to be a good communicator so that the patient is sufficiently informed to make their own decisions. 'Informed consent' is thus a vital precursor to any treatment. A doctor must respect a patient's refusal for treatment even if they think it is not the correct choice. Note that patients cannot demand treatment – only refuse it, e.g. an alcoholic patient, if deemed to have capacity, can refuse rehabilitation but cannot demand a liver transplant.

There are many situations where the application of autonomy can be quite complex, for example:

➢ **Treating children:** Consent is usually required from the parents, although the autonomy of the child is taken into account increasingly as they get older.

➢ **Treating adults without the <u>capacity</u>** to make important decisions. The first challenge with this is in assessing whether or not a patient has the capacity to make the decisions. Just because a patient has a mental illness does not necessarily mean that they lack the capacity to make decisions about their health care. Where patients do lack capacity, the power to make decisions is transferred to the next of kin (or Legal Power of Attorney, if one has been set up).

Justice

This deals with the fair distribution and allocation of healthcare resources for the population. When answering a question on medical ethics, you need to ensure that you show an appreciation for the fact that there are often two sides of the argument. Where appropriate, you should outline both points of view and how they pertain to the main principles of medical ethics and then come to a reasoned judgement.

It is important to know that sometimes the beneficence and autonomy may be in conflict. For example, consider a patient that is refusing treatment that could be lifesaving. It is possible that sometimes the patients make decisions that are not correct or in conflict with beneficence duties of a doctor. When faced with such scenarios, try to understand the reasoning of the patient. Is it because of fear, ignorance or something different, for example religious beliefs. If the decisions of the patients are fully informed and the patient has the capacity to make well-informed decisions (patient is not confused due to illness/drugs or mental illness) then clinicians must respect the autonomy of the patient.

Further important **concepts in medical ethics** include:

Consent

This in a way is an extension of Autonomy: patients have the right to first agree (or refuse) to a procedure, treatment or intervention. For consent to be valid, it must be **a voluntary informed consent.** This means that the patient must have sufficient mental capacity to make the decision and must be presented with all the relevant information (benefits, side effects, and the likely complications) in a way they can understand.

Confidentiality

Patients expect that the information they reveal to doctors will be kept private. This is a key component in maintaining the trust between patients and doctors. You must ensure that patient details are kept confidential. This often comes up in scenarios where relatives may be asking for information about their parent who is a patient (has the patient given you permission to talk to their relative about their condition?) or if a patient/relative tries to have a discussion in the corridor (can you have the discussion in a more private area, less likely to be overheard?). Confidentiality can be broken if you suspect that a patient is a risk to themselves or to others, e.g. terrorism, child abuse, informing the DVLA if a patient is at risk of seizures, road accidents, etc.

Mental Capacity Act

The primary purpose of the 2005 act is to govern the decision-making process on behalf of adults who lack the capacity to make decisions for themselves. There are several principles to be aware of:

1. A person must be assumed to have capacity unless proven otherwise.
2. A person is not to be treated as unable to make a decision unless all practicable steps to help them to do so have been taken without success.
3. A person is not to be treated as unable to make a decision merely because they make an unwise decision.
4. An act must be in their best interest.
5. The act must be the least restrictive with regards to the individual's freedoms.

Capacity

Medical capacity is the patient's ability to make specific decisions about their care. The capacity is time and 'point' specific, meaning that they may not have the capacity to make complex financial decisions, but can make decisions about receiving or declining specific treatment. This can change over time, so there may be a time when they have capacity but other times when they don't (this can fluctuate even within days or hours, depending on their clinical condition). For example, a patient admitted with a severe infection may not have capacity on their first day in hospital but this may change as they improve with treatment.

When assessing capacity, it is important to know that the individual does not have an underlying mental illness or a reason to compromise their decision-making abilities.

Important things to consider are:

➢ Can the patient understand the information?
➢ Can the patient retain the information?
➢ Can they analyse the information correctly?
➢ Can they communicate their choices clearly?

Any deficiency in any of these steps can lead to the patient lacking capacity to make a decision. The understanding of this process is crucial as doctors are often faced with situations where patients may make decisions that are not in keeping with medical advice (e.g. a Jehovah's Witness refusing blood products and having serious blood loss). Carrying out procedures or treatment that directly contravenes a patient's wishes who has capacity is a breach of patient's autonomy, and can be prosecuted.

Doctors should consider a formal mental capacity assessment in the following scenarios:

1. Sudden change in mental status
2. Refusal to treatment, e.g. unclear reason or due to irrational biases/beliefs
3. Known psychiatric/neurologic condition
4. People at extreme of ages < 18 years or > 85 years

Medical Law

Understanding the principles of medical law is also essential for success in certain ethical scenarios. Here is a brief overview of some key legal cases and principles that you should familiarise yourself with:

Mental Health Act

This act basically governs how heath care professionals interact with people with mental disorders, and their rights to enforce investigation treatment. The original act was passed in 1983, but there was a significant amendment in 2007. The most significant components for health professionals are the definition of holding powers, which allow doctors to detain and treat a patient with a mental illness against their will. Most notably, these are the section 5(2) and 5(4) defining doctors' and nurses' duties respectively. Other orders to be aware off are Section 135 (magistrate order) and section 136 (police order), as well as section 2 and section 3 (detention for investigation and treatment, respectively). You should hopefully have covered these during psychiatry teaching in medical school.

Data Protection Act

This act gives the GMC power to control how data is collected, recorded and used. Personal data under the act is defined as identifiable information. It's important that data is:

1) Processed fairly and lawfully
2) Gathered for specific purposes.
3) The data is adequate, relevant, accurate, and kept up to date

This governs how doctors collect patient information and whom they can share this information with. Practical examples are doctors needing to break confidentiality for acts of suspected terrorism and road traffic accidents.

Gillick Competence

Children under the age of 18 can consent to treatment if they are able to understand, weigh up, and decide they want the treatment. However, they cannot refuse treatment until they are 18 years old. For children under 18 with no parent/guardian who aren't Gillick competent, you are able to act 'in their best interest'.

Bolam Test

The Bolam test is a legal rule that assesses the appropriateness of reasonable care in negligence cases involving a skilled professional. The Bolam test states *"If a doctor reaches the standard of a responsible body of medical opinion, he is not negligent"*. In order for someone to be shown to be negligent, it must be established that:
1) There was a duty of care
2) The duty of care was breached
3) The breach directly led to the patient being harmed

Euthanasia

Euthanasia is a deliberate intervention undertaken with the express intention of ending a life to alleviate pain and suffering. The two main types of euthanasia are:

➤ Active Euthanasia: Doctor causes the patient to die, e.g. by injecting poison
➤ Passive Euthanasia: Doctor lets the patient die, e.g. withdrawing life-sustaining treatment, switch off life-supporting machines

Active Euthanasia is classed as murder in the UK and is illegal. Passive euthanasia is legal. You should revise the main arguments for and against active euthanasia.

Ethics in Relation to Medical Research

In advance of the interview, you should give consideration about how the above ethical concepts relate to medical research. Specific ethical areas that are often asked about in relation to medical research in the interviews include:

> **Confidentiality** (consider the need to keep patient information anonymised in studies, and the different steps that must be taken to do so).

> **Data protection** (consider the technical requirements to keep patients information and databases confidential and secure).

> **Consent** (the same important principles detailed above regarding informed consent must be applied when enrolling patients into research trials. Think about the challenges when enrolling patients to Randomised Controlled Trials, when there is a strong chance that they may be allocated to a placebo arm).

> Ethics in regard to **animal experimentation** (it is critically important to reduce any unnecessary suffering of animals that are the subject of medical research, and that only the required number of animals are used. You should look into the different levels of Home Office clearance required).

> Ethics in regard to **stem cell research** (this is another important topic that you need to consider in advance of the interview: think about the various ethical dilemmas when considering at what stage an embryo is considered a human life, and the challenges that brings when performing medical research on embryos).

> **Fair use and allocation of resources** (this is important when considering the allocation of funding for different conditions, and ensuring that funding within specific projects is used appropriately and ethically).

> **Conflicts of interest** and **research funding** (it is critically important to ensure that all potential conflicts of interests are disclosed and that you consider the relevance of these and how they may influence research in an unethical manner).

> The function of **Research Ethics Committees** (these are the committees that review local research project proposals, and you should be familiar with what they are and roughly how they operate. They are an important way to ensure that research proposals satisfy all ethical requirements).

We would advise you look further into each of the above categories so you are familiar with how the core ethical principles apply to each of them prior to the interview. This is a common and significant area for questioning within the AFP interview.

If you would like to undertake more learning in this area, the authors highly recommend the NIHR administered 'Good Clinical Practice' (please see: https://www.nihr.ac.uk/our-research-community/clinical-research-staff/learning-and-development/national-directory/good-clinical-practice/).

Example Ethical Scenarios

1) A leukaemia patient is refusing stem cell treatment on religious grounds. Without the treatment, he has a 20% chance of survival. How would you use your communication skills to deal with this situation?

Paternalistic medicine (the attitude that the doctor always knows best) is no longer accepted as the correct way to practise. It's important to recognise that certain lifestyle decisions can be even more important to patients than their own health. It would be inappropriate to dismiss these choices even though the doctor's focus is on health. From a communication skills perspective, this question is asking you to demonstrate creativity in how you would use your own interpersonal skills to try to resolve the situation. Reaching a compromise between the patient's values and the physician's goals is a frequent conundrum in medicine, so being able to listen to the patient and figure out what is most important to them is an absolutely essential skill.

A Bad Response:

I would override his refusal by getting a court order as he clearly lacks the capacity to make a rational decision about his own care. Therefore, I should act in his best interests as I know from my medical training what is best for the patient, and it would be irresponsible of me not to do my best to treat him.

Response Analysis:

The response is poor and shows a lack of willingness to engage with the patient on his own terms. The court order is unlikely to lead to treatment being enforced either, especially if the patient has the capacity and is over 18. Whilst it is indeed true that doctors should try to do the right thing for their patients, this paternalistic view would be frowned upon in interviews as it makes the assumption that the treatment is what is best for the patient overall. This opinion suggests that the patient has a 'problem' to be 'fixed', rather than a complex combination of ideas, concerns, and expectations. For example, this patient may suffer severe psychological distress from being forced to act against his beliefs. Therefore, is the stem cell treatment really the best option for his health?

A Good Response:

I would firstly try to understand the religious grounds behind his refusal. If there are conflicting opinions within his religion, it might be worth asking if he would like a religious representative (e.g. Chaplain or Rabbi) to visit him and discuss his options sensitively. If the patient is a minor and there is reason to believe he is being coerced rather than making his own decision, or the patient lacks capacity, there may be grounds for going to the court to get permission to treat him. However, at the end of the day, respect for patient autonomy must be paramount. If the patient has capacity and refuses the treatment, we must support his decision and instead treat any symptoms and problems he may have as a result of the refusal of treatment.

Response Analysis:

This is a good response. The first part demonstrates a desire to understand the patient's point of view, an open mind to learn about different cultures and backgrounds, and a willingness to use communication (even via a third party) to work through problems and issues. The second part demonstrates knowledge of the process of consent for minors, but interviewees wouldn't be expected to have an in-depth knowledge of the laws and processes involved in this. The third part of the response is the most important point – respect for the patient's decision also involves treating any problems they may have as a result of their (informed, consented) decisions. This is an essential aspect of medical care that many doctors struggle with.

Overall:

Being sensitive to the patient's motivations and concerns is an important part of being a doctor. This sort of question makes sure that the interviewee has the right attitude towards care that is expected of a modern doctor, and that they understand that 'acting in the patient's best interests' and giving the most efficacious treatment are not necessarily the same thing. It's also important to recognise that if a treatment is rejected, the doctor should give their best efforts to support the patient medically through other means, even if the patient experiences problems as a result of having rejected the therapy.

2) What issues might arise when using a translator to mediate a patient consultation, and as a doctor, how might you overcome these issues?

This question asks about a part of medicine that is rarely discussed but is of increasing importance to clinical medicine in this country. 'Translators', in this case, could mean official in-hospital translators, telephone translators, or could also include multilingual family members who are used for the purposes of translation. Make sure you define this in your answer.

A Bad Response:

It is bad to use a translator in a consultation. For example, the translator might not be able to translate things fully and so information will be missed. Also, time might be wasted trying to find the translator in the first place and this is especially important for busy doctors. There is a chance that the translator might not know medical terminology and so could struggle to relay all the correct information between the patient and doctor.

Response Analysis:

This is a terrible response for several reasons. Firstly, there is very little structure to the answer. The opening is weak, there is then a list of points that are poorly illustrated, and there is no conclusion that brings the points together at the end. Finally, this applicant has made the grave error of not answering both parts of the question. This is a mistake that is often made in the pressure of an interview setting. If you are in an interview and hear an 'and' that is joining two questions together, make sure in your head that you set out to answer both parts. You might structure this as two separate answers or combine answers to both into a single argument.

A Good Response:

In our increasingly multicultural society, the use of translators in medicine is increasingly prevalent and necessary. Many of the usual communication skills and techniques that are used by doctors are rendered useless when the patient does not speak the same language, and a strong patient-doctor relationship can be difficult to establish. Furthermore, in a profession in which strict confidentiality is essential, the use of unofficial translators may be open to abuse and any medical professional should do everything in their power to prevent such abuses.

There is a distinction between in-hospital official translators and when family members are used as translators, as is often the case in clinical medicine. A consultation that requires the use of a translator may not be ideal for either party, however, there are several things that the doctor might do to improve the situation.

Firstly, before beginning the consultation, it is crucial that both the patient and translator understand the format of a translated consultation and are happy to proceed. This is especially true when a family member is used as a translator.

Secondly, it is key that all information is correctly conveyed across the language barrier. This can be achieved in several ways. For example, the doctor might use simple language and easily phrased questions. He/she should also only use short questions and wait for the translator to translate each portion. Finally, the doctor could regularly check and confirm throughout the consultation that the patient understands what is being said and indeed that the doctor has understood everything that the patient has said. Furthermore, there are several pitfalls that might occur during a consultation when using translators, and these pitfalls have the potential to be highly detrimental to the patient's welfare.

One potential issue is presented by the identity of the translator. If the translator is a family member or knows the patient personally, something which is quite likely if they come from the same community, then the patient might be embarrassed to present certain pieces of information that may be of critical importance to the consultation. In addition, the same could apply to the translator through their own embarrassment or ulterior motive. If any of these possibilities are suspected, then the doctor should seek to repeat the consultation with a different translator.

In summary, there are multiple important issues that arise through the use of translators in medicine. However, translators are an absolute necessity in our multicultural society, and therefore, doctors should be well educated on the possible pitfalls that might arise and should know how these can be avoided.

Response Analysis:

This applicant's answer starts with a strong opening that describes the importance of the issue. It then goes on to define what exactly the term 'translator' includes in this context. There is a strong structure with each point being well signposted. As opposed to having two separate answers to the two parts of the question, this applicant has decided to combine the two answers into one narrative. Either is acceptable.

Overall:

Always ensure you answer both parts of a question.

3) You are asked to gain consent from a patient for a procedure. What do you need to consider to ensure that consent is achieved?

As you gain experience throughout your career, you will be asked to take on more responsibilities. One of these responsibilities is taking consent for procedures: whilst you need to be careful that you are not asked to take consent inappropriately, the process of taking consent becomes a reality in the Foundation Programme as you are asked to perform procedures such as catheterisation and nasogastric tube insertion.

A Bad Response:

Consent is very important in modern medicine; without consent, a procedure cannot go ahead. Consent is achieved when the doctor explains what the risks of a procedure are and has checked that the patient is happy to proceed. The issue of consent has many ethical implications. The Hippocratic Oath states that a doctor should do no harm and should act in the patient's best interests. Modern medicine relies on the fact that patients trust the medical profession to provide the very best service. If this trust is undermined, for example, by not following the Hippocratic Oath fully, then the medical profession cannot as effectively serve the population.

Response Analysis:

The key fault that this applicant makes in their answer is that they go off on a tangent about the ethical implications of consent. It is easy to fall into this trap as you may have a confident answer to something very much related to the question being asked, so it is tempting to talk about that even if it is not a direct answer. Always make sure that you structure a very relevant answer to the question that is being asked.

A Good Response:

Consent is a fundamental prerequisite of any procedure in an ethical healthcare system. Before visiting the patient, it is essential that you yourself understand the procedure, why it is being performed on this particular patient, and what the possible risks of the procedure are.

There are several key criteria that must be met to attain consent. Firstly, it is imperative to make sure that the patient fully understands what the procedure involves. For this reason, any explanation of the procedure given by the doctor should not involve medical jargon and should be at a level that the patient can comprehend.

Secondly, the patient must know about the risks involved. Even if a procedure is perfectly explained, this might imply that there aren't possible risks to the procedure and so the patient would not be able to give effective consent. Thirdly, the patient must know what the proposed benefits of the procedure are. Finally, it is crucial that the patient understands what will happen if they do not have the procedure. They may not wish to undertake a daunting procedure, but this might be by far the better of two options. Therefore, to be able to give true consent, it is necessary that the patient understands this.

However, before one can assess these different criteria, it is necessary to check that they can properly process information and that they can actually retain information. This could be done by asking the patient to repeat what you have said so far at various points during the consultation. Furthermore, we must give consideration to the patient's mental state, for instance, if they are not corpus mentis then consent cannot be obtained. This is because a patient who has a psychiatric condition may be able to appear to give consent but this cannot be accepted from an ethical standpoint.

Response Analysis:
The applicant gives an excellent answer to the question. There is a strong opening, followed by clearly structured key points that are a direct answer to the question. The applicant then goes into further detail by explaining pitfalls that could arise if we just followed the basic formula of consent.

Overall:
A key learning point in this example is to always make sure that you directly answer the question. This is a question about what informed consent is – not an ethical dilemma!

4) You're given £1 Million to spend on either an MRI machine or on 50 liver transplants for patients with alcoholic liver disease (cirrhosis). Which one would you choose?

Decisions about resource allocation are hugely important in a system like the NHS where resources are so limited and those making the decisions must be able to justify them to the public. Analysis of the cost-effectiveness of treatments is done by NICE, which assesses how money can be best spent to achieve the best for the most people. This uses measures such as QALYs (Quality Adjusted Life Years). The other ethical decision here is whether patients should be treated for arguably self-inflicted conditions.

A Bad Response:
I would pay for the MRI machine. This is because for the patients with alcoholic cirrhosis, their condition is self-inflicted and so they should be given less priority than patients whose diseases are not self-inflicted, like many of those who would be helped by the new MRI machine.

Response Analysis:
This alludes to a common ethical debate about whether, in a resource-limited public health system like the NHS, those with conditions which could be considered self-inflicted should be given less priority than other patients or perhaps be asked to pay for their healthcare. The arguments put forward for this include the idea that this would discourage people from unhealthy or risky lifestyle choices and so remove some of the burdens that these patients present to the NHS, while also benefitting the patients themselves. In contrast, arguments against this state that in many cases the causes of a disease can be multi-factorial, including lifestyle risk factors but also genetic predisposition for the disease, so it cannot be said with complete certainty that a person's lifestyle choices are responsible for the disease. Furthermore, such a move would represent a slippery slope towards doctors making dangerous judgements about which patients are worth treating and which are not. What makes this answer bad is that the candidate has failed to support their decision with an ethical argument or to recognise that their valid counter-arguments to his position. Furthermore, the candidate hasn't shown any awareness about how these resource allocation decisions are really made.

A Good Response:

I suppose my decision would have to depend on a number of factors. To start, I would want to know if there has been any analysis from NICE regarding which of these options has the potential to contribute to the most QALYs. While liver transplants make a relatively quantifiable improvement to the recipients' lives, it is difficult to quantify the amount of benefit from using an MRI machine – use of the machine does not generate QALYs in itself, but the earlier and more accurate diagnosis that it can offer certainly has the potential to do so. Another factor would, of course, have to be the relative need for MRI machines vs. liver transplants. For example, giving a hospital a second MRI machine will be of substantially more benefit than giving it its sixth MRI machine. Ultimately, I think this approach would probably lead me to opt for the MRI machine. This is because, although the liver transplants are of very obvious and substantial benefit to the 50 people who get the transplant, the MRI machine has the potential to last for decades and so help thousands of patients so that its cumulative contribution to wellbeing is perhaps greater.

Response Analysis:

This answer shows that the candidate has an idea about the process behind resource allocation decisions in the NHS and the role of NICE. It is also a thoughtful approach to the problems of working out how to fairly compare very different types of expenses, such as diagnostic tool versus a treatment. It is good that the candidate ultimately picks one of the options as the question explicitly asks for this and their choice is supported by the caveats that it would require deeper analysis and rely on an evidence-base.

Overall:

What matters more is not whether you pick the MRI machine or the liver transplants but your ability to give a balanced and rational ethical argument to support your answer, to demonstrate relevant knowledge and consider the practicalities of applying this in the real world.

5) What are the main principles of medical ethics? Which one is most important?

There are a few principles that are generally accepted as the core of medical ethics. It can be useful to read a little about them to make sure you have a good grasp on what they mean. See the Medical Ethics section for more details.

In answering this question, good answers will not just state what the main principles of medical ethics are, but why they are so important. You don't need to go into too much detail, just show that you know what the principles mean. In choosing which principle is most important, it is good to show balanced reasoning in your answer, i.e. that you recognise that any single one of the principles could be argued to be the most important but for specific reasons you have picked this one.

A Bad Response:
It is really important for doctors to empathise with their patients, so empathy is probably the main principle. If doctors empathise with their patients, this means they will do what is in the patients' best interests, so it is the most important principle in medical ethics.

Response Analysis:
Empathy is obviously an important component of the doctor-patient relationship and the ability to empathise is crucial for all medical professionals, but it is in itself not a principle of medical ethics. The candidate seems to be getting at the idea of beneficence but does not really explain what they mean or why it is so important. If you are asked to make a judgement on which medical principle is most important, it is a good idea to have mentioned other medical principles earlier in your answer to compare it to. Thus the main way in which this answer falls down is in having shown no real appreciation for so many of the medical principles mentioned above.

A Good Response:

The main principles of medical ethics are usually said to be beneficence, non-maleficence, autonomy and justice. It is very difficult to say which is most important as, by definition, they are each crucial in medicine and they are all very linked with each other. For example, if a patient wants a treatment that a resource-limited health system, like the NHS, can't offer without compromising the healthcare to someone else then this is a conflict between autonomy and justice. If I had to pick, I would say that beneficence is probably the most important principle as if it is applied to all your patients then it should imply justice and if a patient is properly respected, then it should also take into account the importance of autonomy.

Response Analysis:

This candidate showed knowledge in both the main principles and understanding of what they mean and how they could be applied practically. Notice how this candidate showed their understanding without actually defining each principle, though there wouldn't necessarily have been anything wrong with doing so. This candidate recognised the difficulty in picking a 'most important' principle, in so doing showing balance and humility. Their insight into the conflict between different principles further shows a good understanding and suggests they have given medical ethics a good degree of thought.

Overall:

This question can be a really easy one if you familiarise yourself with the main principles of medical ethics so that you know you can define them and recognise how they might apply in a clinical setting. The question of which is 'most important' has no single right answer – it can be good to say this and then make sure you have a reasonable justification for whichever principle you pick.

6) When can doctors break confidentiality?

As doctors, we have an ethical & legal obligation to protect patient information. This improves patient-doctor trust. However, there are circumstances when doctors are required to break patient confidentiality, such as:

➢ The patient is very likely to cause harm to others, e.g. mental health disorder
➢ Patient doesn't have the capacity, e.g. infants
➢ Social Service input is required, e.g. child abuse
➢ At request of police, e.g. if a patient is suspected of terrorism
➢ Inability to safely operate a motor vehicle, e.g. epilepsy
➢ Notifiable diseases

A Bad Response:
Doctors can break confidentiality when they believe that it will benefit the patient. Confidentiality is an important aspect of medical care because it protects patients from having information that is private to them being disclosed to the public. Confidentiality can also immediately be broken if a patient who has been advised not to drive is found to be driving as it causes a risk to the public if the driver is involved in an accident.

Response Analysis:
The first sentence in this response is a little vague; ideally, the candidate would expand on how exactly breaking confidentiality would benefit the patient. For example, is it because the patient in question is in grave danger from abuse, threatened by a weapon, or details about them need to be disclosed in order to catch the criminal? The question does, however, appreciate the importance of maintaining confidentiality. To state that confidentiality can be broken immediately without first consulting the patient (as in the driving scenario) and advising them of disclosing information themselves is technically inaccurate.

A Good Response:

Patients have a right to expect their doctors to maintain confidentiality and doing so is very important to maintain a good patient-doctor relationship as well as maintain the public's trust in the profession. However, there are a number of circumstances under which doctors may break confidentiality. As stated in the GMC guidance, it may be broken if it is required by the law, if it is in the public's best interest due to a communicable disease such as Measles (also required, as this is a notifiable disease) or a serious crime needing to be reported such as a gunshot wound. It is always important to ask patients first if their information can be disclosed and to encourage them to disclose things themselves. For example, if a person with uncontrolled epilepsy is driving, you have a duty to report it to the DVLA but you must give the patient every chance to tell the DVLA about their condition themselves. In this case, you can only break confidentiality if the patient refuses to inform the DVLA so that you can protect them and the general public.

Response Analysis:

The response identifies the importance of maintaining confidentiality. The candidate nicely references an appropriate source for doctors such as the GMC to state instances in which confidentiality is broken. This shows that the candidate has read the guidance that doctors are expected to know and is able to apply their knowledge to answer this question. The examples are accurate.

Overall:

It is important to be familiar with key 'hot topics' in medicine such as consent and confidentiality and to carry out a little background reading on these prior to attending a medical interview in order to provide them with accurate examples. Examiners will indeed be impressed if you understand these core concepts and their importance to medical practice. The GMC website's 'good medical practice' is a very good site to visit in order to obtain further information on these topics and others that are likely to be assessed in your interviews.

Professionalism Scenario

Any professionalism scenario that comes up is often interlinked with an ethical scenario, but for the purposes of this book we will discuss them separately to ensure that the core principles that need to be covered in each are not missed.

The most important guiding principle in the professionalism scenario is that you must aim to prevent patient harm, and therefore protect patient safety, at all costs. This means that the most important focus of your answer will be to ensure that your actions safeguard the health of patients: whether this means removing drunk colleagues from clinical areas, or staying late to ensure appropriate handover of a sick patient.

Following establishment of how you would act to preserve patient safety, you can then dissect the rest of the case and discuss how you would act as a professional in each situation. Think back to the Situational Judgement Test: the principles you applied there are exactly the same as you need to apply here.

Situational Judgment: A Refresher

The Situational Judgement Test assessed your ability to prioritise competing demands and resolve disputes in a harmonious manner.

When faced with a situational question, it is helpful to use a basic framework:
1. Identify the basic dilemma
2. Identify your potential courses of action
3. Consider the advantages & disadvantages of each option you're given
4. Consider any alternative solutions, i.e. options outside the ones you are given
5. Think about how the perspectives of colleagues and patients may differ from your own
6. Balance these to pick an action that you can justify with a logical argument

Read "Tomorrow's Doctors" and "Good Medical Practice"

These are publications produced by the General Medical Council (GMC) which can be found on their website. The GMC regulate the medical profession to ensure that standards remain high. These publications can be found on their website. Reading through this ensures you have the required principles at the forefront of your answers.

Hierarchy

The patient is of **primary importance**. All decisions that affect patient care should be made to benefit the patient. Of **secondary importance** are your work colleagues. So if there is no risk to patients, you should help out your colleagues and avoid doing anything that would undermine them or harm their reputation – but if doing so would bring detriment to any patient, then the patient's priorities come to the top. Finally, of **lowest importance** is yourself. You should avoid working outside hours and strive to further your education, but not at the expense of patients or your colleagues.

There are several core principles that you should attempt to apply to SJT questions that will help your decision making:

Adopt a Patient-Centred Approach to Care

This involves being able to treat patients as individuals and respecting their decisions. You should also respect a patient's right to confidentiality unless there is a significant risk to the general public. The most important principle is to **never compromise patient safety**.

Working Well in a Team

Teamwork is an essential part of any job. You must be a trustworthy and reliable team member and also communicate effectively within the team. You should support your senior and junior colleagues should they require it. It is important to avoid conflict and be able to de-escalate situations without jeopardising professional relationships where possible.

Commitment to Professionalism

You should always act with honesty and integrity as this is expected of anyone entering the profession. This includes apologising for your mistakes and trying to ensure other people apologise for theirs.

Taking Responsibility for your learning

Medicine is a career where you are continuously learning. You are the sole person responsible for it and you will need to prioritise your jobs to ensure you attend scheduled teaching and courses. You should be able to critically reflect upon your experiences.

Example Situational Judgement Questions

Example A:

"The ward nurse informs you that one of your FY1 colleagues is taking morphine from the drug cabinet. What do you do?"

This question is not about your knowledge of morphine but about what to do if someone you know is reported to be doing something that is not correct. The obvious trap here is to say, *"I would go speak to the doctor and inform their boss."*

This would be a very serious accusation; remember that the nurse may be wrongly informed, biased or have a grudge against that doctor. Before you do anything, you must show that you will find out the facts and establish whether this is a recurring problem or not and if there are any obvious explainable reasons for it.

Thus, although the question might appear to be very simple, it actually tests multiple skills. It's important to consider the implications of your actions rather than launch into an answer straight away.

"Reports of a colleague taking medication from a patient's drug cabinet are clearly extremely concerning. Before I do anything, I would try to establish the facts by talking to others who may be in a position to observe such behaviour. This will ensure that it removes any reporter's personal bias or perceptions. If this is true, I would offer to speak to the colleague in private and ask their views. I would offer my support by covering their work to ensure that patient safety is not compromised, and would ask them to leave the clinical area and talk to their educational supervisor as a matter of urgency. I would encourage them to get external help, and I would involve my seniors if I felt that the situation wasn't resolving."

Example B:

You are just finishing a busy shift on the Acute Assessment Unit (AAU). Your FY1 colleague who is due to replace you for the evening shift leaves a message with the nurse in charge that he will be 15 to 30 minutes late. There is only a 30-minute overlap between your timetables to handover to your colleague. You need to leave on time as you have a social engagement to attend with your partner.

Rank the following actions in response to this situation in ascending order of appropriateness:

A. Make a list of the patients under your care on the AAU, detailing their outstanding issues, leaving this on the doctor's office notice board when your shift ends and then leave at the end of your shift.

B. Quickly go around each of the patients on the AAU, leaving an entry in the notes highlighting the major outstanding issues relating to each patient and then leave at the end of your shift.

C. Make a list of patients and outstanding investigations to give to your colleague as soon as he arrives.

D. Ask your registrar if you can leave a list of your patients and their outstanding issues with him to give to your colleague when he arrives and then leave at the end of your shift.

E. Leave a message for your partner explaining that you will be 30 minutes late.

This question gives you the opportunity to demonstrate a conscientious attitude by prioritising patient care over personal concerns and team working. It would be unfair on your colleague to not give them the opportunity to ask any questions about the handover. The safest option is (E) as it ensures a comprehensive handover and doesn't sacrifice patient safety. The other options all involve a non-verbal handover, which risks patient safety.

If you weren't given these options, you could instead talk the interviewer through your reasoning:
"So to summarise, I am faced with the situation where I am finishing my shift and the doctor taking over is running late. If I overstay, I will be late for my social commitment. If I leave, the handover will be inefficient and important information relevant to patient care may not get passed on.

In this situation, I have the option to write all the remaining tasks on paper and either give them to another person that is coming in to pass on to the next person or leave it in an office for the attention of the incoming doctor. This is not the best option as there is a risk that the information may not get passed on at all or not in a timely manner, which could compromise patient care.

I feel the best option would be for me to call my partner to let them know that I will be running late and wait for the incoming doctor to do a face-to-face handover"

Many applicants find the Mnemonic *INSIST* helpful when structuring their answers:

IN	• Seek **IN**formation • Find out if the information you have is correct
S	• Patient & People **S**afety • Ensure noone has/will come to harm
I	• **I**nteract with Person • Don't be confrontational
S	• **S**upport the Person • Be Empathetic
T	• Involve other **T**eam Members • Involve seniors if things don't improve

We now discuss some specific examples of scenarios that are likely to appear during a scenario on professionalism. We cover the main principles required to answer them successfully, and give advice on what not to include in these answers.

Example Professionalism Scenarios

1) You are a junior doctor on cardiology. Your consultant in charge turns up on Monday morning smelling strongly of alcohol. What do you do?

This question tests your ability to deal with a senior colleague whom you suspect is drinking alcohol and has turned up to work smelling of alcohol. There is usually a pattern to follow when answering these questions: try to approach the person in question to gather a bit of information: are they, in fact, drinking alcohol? You may have been mistaken and it would, therefore, be wrong to take any further action. Next, you should try and explore the reason behind their behaviour: is it a transient and short-lasting event that has caused the consultant to drink? If so, hopefully there shouldn't be a long-term issue here. Thirdly, the interviewer would like to hear that you are taking steps to ensure that patients are safe. This may involve asking the consultant politely to get some rest and go home: clinical errors or prescribing errors due to alcohol consumption could potentially be deadly. They will want to know what you would do if the consultant declined. Lastly, you may want to suggest the consultant seek some help.

A Bad Response:

Smelling strongly of alcohol at your workplace is, in my opinion, unacceptable. The consultant, although a senior figure, should know better and I think his behaviour should be reported promptly. The consequences of having a drunken consultant in the clinical area are unsafe and it also tarnishes the doctors' reputation as a whole. I would therefore ask my registrar to have a word with the consultant and hopefully, the matter will be escalated to the medical director who can then decide the best course of action.

Response Analysis:

This candidate is rather rash in his/her approach to the situation. Firstly, there is only a suspicion that the consultant is drinking alcohol. It is thus better to sensitively explore this first before discussing the situation with anybody else. Reporting somebody without first getting the facts straight is inappropriate. Whilst you can seek help from your registrar who will be senior to you, the answer here sounds more like you are passing the buck to the registrar and asking them to sort the situation out rather than seeking advice and acting on the advice yourself; interviewers will appreciate you being proactive and sorting matters out yourself.

A Good Response:

This is a complex scenario. As there is only a presumption here that the consultant has been drinking (he smells of alcohol only), I would approach him and politely ask him if he has been drinking any alcohol. I would next offer to explore his behaviour by asking him what has led him to drink alcohol and what has led him to still smell of it when he comes into work. I would then suggest he takes the rest of the day off after ensuring his shift is covered by explaining that patient safety may be compromised if he practices medicine under the influence. If he refused to do this, I would contact my educational supervisor for urgent advice. Lastly, I would suggest to him that he seeks further help, either by going to his GP or going to occupational health.

Response Analysis:

This answer takes a calm and measured approach to the situation by following the 'usual' steps for this type of scenario. The candidate is information gathering rather than reporting the consultant straight away. There is also an awareness that patient safety may be at risk, and the candidate provides a solution to tackle this and understands the need to be sensitive here.

Overall:

Professionalism questions such as this can be difficult, and the key is to take a measured and calm approach to the situation. Reporting individuals straight away before attempting to resolve the situation between teams is often not the right approach, and interviewers would rather you to talk to the person in question yourself and take it from there. But remember that patient safety is the most important aspect here and if the consultant were to refuse to go home and continue seeing patients under the influence, you may then need to escalate the situation to someone more senior to you to ensure that patients are not in danger.

2) You're on a busy on call admission shift with your registrar who tells you that he feels 'fed up and just wants to end it all'. You know he has gone through a difficult divorce and is on anti-depressants. What would you do?

This question aims to assess your ability to take the correct steps to effectively deal with a complex scenario. Approach this situation like the other professionalism questions in this book: discuss the person in question's feelings, ensure patient safety is maintained, and advise the person to seek help.

A Bad Response:

This is a rather tricky question. I'm not sure exactly what I would do: perhaps I would like to ask my fellow colleagues what they would do if they were in my shoes. I am quite concerned that the registrar wants to 'end it all', but it is a busy shift. I think he should have called in sick if he didn't feel like working today. I could speak to the consultant about him because he is in charge and, therefore, should be able to deal with the situation effectively. Or perhaps his medication has not been titrated enough? Maybe I can advise him to increase the dose of his medication and see if that makes him feel better?

Response Analysis:

It is important to support your colleagues through difficult times and act compassionate towards them, just like you would with any patient. Therefore, try to listen to them and help them out rather than worry about how busy A+E is. Whilst asking fellow colleagues for advice is good practice, it may be that the registrar has come to you in confidence and would not want you to discuss his situation with others. Also, remember that it is better for you to suggest for the registrar to raise the issue with their consultant rather than you raising it. The registrar will be in a much better position to explain his/her situation than you will. It is dangerous to ask him to increase the dose of his medication - this should be left to the person who prescribes the medication, as they will have information about his other medical conditions and know if it is indeed safe to increase the dose. In this way, it may have been more appropriate to ask the registrar to seek help from his/her own doctor.

A Good Response:

This is a difficult situation but this is how I would approach it. I would firstly suggest to the registrar to move to a quieter room to explore his feelings further. Before doing this, I would ensure there is adequate staff cover and inform the nurses of our temporary absence on the ward. I would assess whether I felt the patient's low mood meant that he was a risk to patient safety, and if so would advise he took the rest of the shift off. From the scenario, it seems as if his low mood is poorly controlled on the current medication and I would, therefore, advise him to book an appointment to see his GP. Furthermore, I would advise him to discuss his issues and concerns with his educational supervisor, as they will be experienced in dealing with pastoral care issues.

Response Analysis:

This answer demonstrates a good understanding of the necessary steps to deal with a complex scenario. It shows that it is important to discuss the registrar's feelings with him, not only to provide colleague support, but also to understand how severe the low mood is in order to establish whether he is able to continue with work and not compromise patient safety. It also nicely highlights that communicating with the nurse and ensuring the shift is covered is very important. The answer also provides longer-term management options and offers the registrar further advice on who to turn to for further help.

Overall:

Try not to discuss sensitive issues with your peers (so spreading 'gossip') but rather try and discuss it with the person in question directly. If you cannot find a solution, then ask him/her to escalate the situation to the consultant in charge. Remember, patient safety is critical important here and if the registrar is too depressed to work, he/she will need to step out of the clinical area. Lastly, remember there are a number of people in the hospital that are trained to help doctors with these types of issues.

3) You are faced with a patient's angry relatives. The patient is sleeping poorly and complains that the ward staff are ignoring her. She is very tearful. What do you do?

Sometimes hospitals can fail in their care and complaints are made. Lack of time and attention paid to patients means that serious mistakes can be made. Medical staff may not have enough time with each individual patient, and so their full medical and emotional needs may not be met. Patients can be left in a high state of anxiety because staff do not have time to talk to them enough.

It is important to take a holistic approach to patient management (consider the whole person, meaning their physical, emotional, mental, and spiritual health).

The key skill needed for dealing with angry patients or relatives is communication, but you must do so in a professional manner, and therefore this type of scenario can also appear in the professionalism interview.

A Bad Response:

1) I would apologise profusely and make time to spend with the patient.

2) I can understand why the relatives were angry. However, I would explain that the staff are very busy at the moment, and that they will assist the patient as soon as they were available.

Response Analysis:

In the first answer, the candidate misses the complex nature of the situation by simply stating they would 'make time'. As you will have no doubt experienced already, carving out time is not easy. The second answer is almost the opposite. It is likely to anger the relatives. The lack of apology and the rush to defend the service gives an impression of lack of empathy. Empathy is an essential quality in a doctor and it is important to acknowledge and address the relatives' concerns.

A Good Response:

Good communication skills are key to fulfilling a doctor's role. This includes listening. I would first apologise and then listen to the relatives concerns, trying to find out more about the situation – is the patient more concerned about the lack of attention or the reduced sleep? I would then work with the relatives and patient to address the patient's primary concern – partnership between healthcare professionals and patients is important in order to produce a patient centred culture in the NHS.

Response Analysis:

This answer has a better structure. It begins by very quickly getting to the point of the question – interviewers want to know about your communication skills. By acknowledging this early, the interviewers know you are aware of the key issue in this question. The candidate also shows a caring and reflective nature by realising that there may be more than one reason for the patient's emotional state (*'is the patient more concerned about the lack of attention or the reduced sleep?'*). Using the phrase *'partnership between healthcare professionals and patients'* shows the candidate is aware of the need for joint decision making between the patient and doctor, which is a cornerstone of good communication skills.

Overall:

A good answer will show empathy and showcase your communication skills. It is important to remember that healthcare professionals work together with patients to deliver optimum care.

4) You are just about to finish your work for the day when the ward nurse asks you to talk to the angry sister of a patient who is admitted under a different team. You have a dinner date with your partner and need to drive to the restaurant. What would you do?

This question is about dealing with an angry relative as well as balancing work and social plans. It also tests your time and people management skills. Your response to stress will also be assessed. If you don't leave in time, you will be late.

A Bad Response:

I would say to the nurse that I had finished for the day and as this was not my patient anyway that she should call someone else to speak with the relative.

Response Analysis:

The trainee comes across as someone who shirks from responsibility and has a lack of empathy. They fail to actually find out what the problem is from the nurse. This is important because simple issues can be quickly resolved, e.g. analgesia if the brother was in lots of pain. This would mean that the ward nurse wouldn't be left with an angry relative. Although it's important that you take your breaks as a doctor and leave on time, it's also important not to neglect your duties.

A Good Response:

This patient is not on my team but is being managed by Dr Smith's team. I would aim to find out what the problem is. If it is something quick maybe I could talk to the relative, and if it requires more discussion I'd advise her to make an appointment to see Dr Smith who is the responsible consultant. I can also bleep someone in Dr Smith's team so that they can explain this to the sister. If this is clinically urgent, I am happy to stay behind but I'll need to make a quick call to my fiancée to explain that I'll be late.

Response Analysis:

Answering this way, you have demonstrated that you will be a hard-working doctor that will work well in a team, does not get stressed with unexpected situations, empathises well, and are able to take extra steps to ensure your patients' welfare is maintained at all times. It shows that you know what would be required in similar circumstances where leaving early may put patient safety at risk.

Overall:

In such scenarios, it is useful to ensure that your actions don't compromise patient safety (in life and death situations you can't walk away). If someone wants to know about the progress of the family member, you should be able to spend a few minutes (if it is a quick discussion) to diffuse the situation and offer to get someone else from the parent team to have an in-depth discussion. In some ways, it is irrelevant that the patient is from a different team as the on-call doctor is also unlikely to be from the same team.

5) What is clinical governance? Why is it important?

Clinical governance refers to the systematic approach used by NHS Trusts to maintain and improve the quality of patient care within the health service. Prior to the introduction of clinical governance, NHS Trusts were responsible only for the financial management of their organisation and it was the responsibility of individual health care professionals to maintain high standards of care. Nowadays, each trust (alongside the individual clinicians) is responsible for maintaining the highest possible standard of care and doing so in the safest possible manner. The best answers to this question will demonstrate how effective clinical governance is achieved and in doing so will explain its importance.

A Bad Response:

Clinical governance is the process by which NHS Trusts ensure that their health care provision is delivered in the most efficient way. In a time when cuts to healthcare budgets are commonplace, trusts have to find new ways to cut spending while still providing an appropriate level of care. The cornerstone of clinical governance is finding the most cost-effective methods to serve the local population.

Response Analysis:

This answer shows a lack of understanding of clinical governance. Clinical governance refers only to the process by which trusts ensure the highest standard of clinical care. Cost-effectiveness of treatments may form part of clinical governance but financial factors are not the focus of clinical governance. It should be noted that trusts are under increasing pressure to control spending but this is not the same as clinical governance.

A Good Response:

Clinical governance is the systematic approach used by NHS Trusts to maintain and improve the quality of patient care within the health service. It comprises several different components. The trust and clinicians are together responsible for continued professional development so that all professional knowledge is up to date. The trust must commit to clinical audit/quality improvement in which clinical practice is reviewed, altered and reassessed, and also to make decisions surrounding clinical practice based on clinical effectiveness. Effectiveness can take into consideration things like value for money and QALYs. Trusts also commit to evidence-based medicine and to find ways to introduce new research into practice in a way that reduces the lag between new discoveries and a reduction in associated morbidities.

In order to ensure proper clinical governance is possible, trusts commit to collect high-quality data on their processes and to allow this data to be openly scrutinised in order that bad practice cannot continue unnoticed.

Ultimately, clinical governance is important in creating systems in which bad practice is stamped out and excellent practice is able to flourish.

Response Analysis:

This is a very thorough answer that explains the mechanisms by which clinical governance is achieved. Crucially, this answer demonstrates an understanding that every mechanism is put in place with the main priority of achieving the highest standard of clinical care.

Overall:

To summarise, clinical governance is about the NHS trust taking appropriate steps to provide the 'right care to the right patients, at the right time, by the right people in the right place'. This is done by ensuring that staff remain up-to-date, perform regular audits and quality improvement projects, implement evidence-based medicine, and have sufficient opportunity to learn from mistakes.

DATA ANALYSIS

Any interview for a clinical-academic position is likely to focus on some form of data analysis. This is a way for the interviewers to assess your critical thinking and reasoning skills, and see how you perform under some form of pressure provided by the questions. Likely areas to come up include population demographic graphs or results from clinical trials. Clearly, it is not possible to cover all the potential topics or examples that can come up, and so we will first discuss some key concepts when answering this type of question before turning to some important general topics and finally a couple of specific examples to allow you to gain further understanding of what the interview may be like.

How to Answer Questions About Data

Many candidates find answering questions about scientific data to be challenging: and rightfully so! After all, you are typically being put under pressure to answer questions and come to conclusions about topics you likely have never seen before. However, there are certain important techniques that you can apply to improve your answers in this station:

1. Take time to think before you answer! Don't worry leaving a gap before you start to talk after being asked the question. Contrary to what you might think, this doesn't look unprofessional but shows confidence and shows that you care and want to answer the question to the best of your ability.

2. Describe what you see. Don't be afraid to begin answering a seemingly complex question with a description of what you are looking at: this is a graph of X plotted against Y, and shows that as Y increases, X also increases. By doing this, you may reveal to yourself the specific answer that the examiners are looking for, and if not at least it shows that you know what to look for when presented with unfamiliar data.

3. In relation to the previous answer: do not forget to read both the title of the table/graph and the axes. You will be surprised at the number of candidates who are asked to present what they see to the examiners but are unable to state what the overall topic of what they were look at was because they forgot to read the title.

4. Be careful with statistics. Statistics is a tricky topic, and many applicants find it as such. Often, when a result is statistically significant there will be a star on the graph or some identification of a P value being less than 0.05. It is important to try to not use the word 'significant' when you mean 'obvious' or 'observable': it is a pet peeve of certain examiners when candidates say a result is significantly different from another when there is no P value listed.

5. In addition, it is useful to familiarise yourself with a variety of statistical terms before the interview, including but not limited to Mean, Median, Odds Ratio, Hazard Ratio, P values, confidence intervals and number needed to treat.

Hierarchy of Evidence

It is important to consider the different types of evidence that can be used when either making decisions about patient care or when performing a literature review of a certain topic. These vary from anecdotal evidence all the way to meta-analyses. We will not describe each type of study in depth as that is beyond the scope of this book, but we will show you the hierarchy below. Any study type you are unfamiliar with you should read up more about prior to the interview.

1. Expert Opinion (WEAKEST)

2. Case Reports

3. Case-control Studies

4. Cohort Studies

5. Controlled Studies

6. Randomised Controlled Studies

7. Systematic Reviews

8. Meta-analyses (STRONGEST)

As mentioned, ensure you are familiar with what each type of evidence listed above is, and ensure you know what the strengths and weakness of each include. A helpful article covering this is: Besen J and Gan SD, A Critical Evaluation of Clinical Research Study Designs (2014). *Journal of Investigative Dermatology* **134**, e18, doi:10.1038/jid.2013.545

Appraising Randomised Controlled Trials

Randomised controlled trials are the gold-standard for comparing different treatments of a specific condition. They are therefore frequently an area of questioning in the AFP interview. Thoughts you should be having when appraising the study prior to answering questions about it include:

- Did the study ask a specific and set question?

- Were patients randomised, and were all participants blinded?

- What was the treatment being compared to (placebo? Previous standard of care?)

- Were all patients that entered the study accounted for?

- Demographically, were the two treatment groups similar at the start of the study?

- What was the size of the treatment effect?

- Are there other possible reasons for the observed effect not mentioned?

Example Data Analysis Questions

We will now illustrate a several examples of graphs / data that are similar to the types of topics that can come up in the AFP interview. Please note: the graphs shown below have been artificially produced to illustrate our educational points and are not clinically accurate, and so should not be treated as such. They are deliberately vague as to which condition they are referring to: this is because their purpose is to show you how to think about data when you are not necessarily familiar with the underlying condition.

We will show the graph on the first page, and will then list the answers on the following page to allow you the opportunity to quiz yourself and see how you do.

Example 1:

Questions:
1. What does this graph show?
2. What may have happened at B?
3. Given your answer to the previous question, what might be the reason for the gradual decline in incidence shown by A?
4. What does C show? Why might this be?
5. What do you understand by the concept of herd immunity?

Answers:

1. What does this graph show?

   This is a graph showing the incidence of new viral cases (of an undisclosed viral illness) per 100,000 population over time. The graph shows an initial downward trend, followed by a significant drop off in the number of cases to almost zero, followed at the very end of the graph by an increased again in the number of cases.

2. What may have happened at B?

   B indicates a sharp decline in the number of new cases of this particular viral illness. There are a number of possible reasons for this including new treatment for the disease or improved public sanitation, but given the extremely sharp reduction in incidence this implies something like a new vaccination scheme taking effect.

3. Given your answer to the previous question, what might be the reason for the gradual decline in incidence shown by A?

   The arrow A points to a section of the graph that shows a gradual decline in the incidence of this viral illness. This could again be caused by a number of reasons, but given the slow reduction over time this implies a more gradual process is at play. Possible causes include improved public education, and improved sanitation.

4. What does C show? Why might this be?

   The arrow C points to a section of the graph that illustrates a small but sharp increase in the number of viral cases from a level close to zero to a small but obvious level of incidence. A number of factors could contribute to this, including a mutation within the virus rendering it somehow resistant to vaccination or treatment. However, given what I know of recent stories in the media, it is possible that fewer and fewer people were vaccinated leading to small outbreaks of the virus. An example of this has occurred recently with the Measles virus, after a study was published in the Lancet claiming links between the vaccination and autism (links which have subsequently not shown to exist). However, the coverage of this study led to a reduction in vaccination and subsequent increase in the number of cases.

5. What do you understand by the concept of herd immunity?

    Herd immunity refers to a term that quantifies the percentage of a population that must be vaccinated against a specific virus for outbreaks of that virus to be inhibited. As the levels of vaccination uptake drop, the percentage of the population immunised has the potential to drop to a level below herd immunity, which in turn may result outbreaks of the virus.

Top Tip! Be factual and objective in your answers: look at the answer to Question 3. The candidate successfully **describes** what the arrow A points to (i.e. "a section of the graph that shows a gradual decline"). This both shows the interviewers that you think objectively and accurately, and gives you time to think about the reasons that may explain what you're describing.

Example 2:

Forest Plot

Studies showing the effect of an intervention:

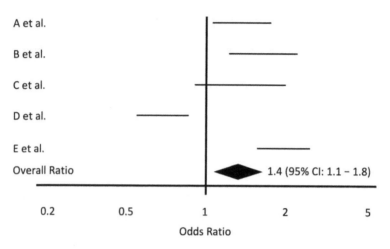

Questions:

1. What do the studies A, B and E have in common

2. What does study C show?

3. Can you suggest any reasons for this?

4. What does study D show?

5. How might you account for this difference?

6. What does the overall Odds Ratio and Confidence Interval suggest?

7. This plot shows the results of a number of different clinical trials. What do you know about the different levels or 'phases' of clinical trials?

Answers:

The answer to these questions implies some prior understanding of Forest plots: and we realise some candidates may not be familiar with them! That is, of course, the major reason for including this question (you may well be presented with a type of graph you are unfamiliar with!), but we will cover now some of the critical parts of the topic of Forest plots.

Forest plots are graphs that are frequently presented in systematic reviews and meta-analyses, and allow the combination and comparison of multiple clinical trials. The horizontal lines illustrate the responses seen in individual clinical trials (in this example, A et al., B et al., etc) and specifically shows the 95% confidence interval of the specific trial. This can be compared to the scale on the bottom, which shows the odds ratio for the specific intervention (which may be a new drug, surgery or other treatment). So, if a trial has an odds ratio entirely greater than 1, then it suggests that that trial has shown a statistically significant improvement (or increase in whatever the odds ratio represents). Finally, the Overall Ratio represents an average of all of the trials included within the Forest plot.

1. What do the studies A, B and E have in common
   The studies A, B and E all have a 95% confidence interval entirely above 1. This implies that the specific intervention of the trial had a statistically significant effect.

2. What does study C show?
   Study C as a 95% confidence interval that overlaps the value of 1. This indicates that the trial may not have arrived at a statistically significant conclusion as to the effect of the intervention: the interval suggests that the true odds ratio may be greater or less than 1.

3. Can you suggest any reasons for this?
   Reasons for this include the possibility of a different demographic population compared to the other studies, or may include flaws in the study (too few patients enrolled) or problems in the running of the study (too many patients dropping out or other potential biases), which may in turn have led to a reduction in the reliability of the results.

4. What does study D show?

   In contrast, study D has a 95% confidence interval entirely below 1. This suggests that it came to the opposite conclusion of studies A, B and E i.e. the intervention had no effect or had less of an effect compared to the comparative measurement (e.g. placebo).

5. How might you account for this difference?

   This difference can be explained by a number of possible reasons. These include the fact that this study was likely carried out on an entirely different population than the other studies, and so I would like to know more about the demographics of this population. Other possibilities include that the study was designed in a significantly different way, or there was some confounding bias that provided significantly different results to the other trials.

6. What does the overall odds ratio and confidence interval suggest

   The overall odds ratio is 1.4 (95% confidence interval 1.1 – 1.8). This implies that the average of the included trials has shown an increase in the odds ratio for this specific intervention. This suggests that the intervention has been successful when investigating the odds of this particular outcome occurring.

7. This plot shows the results of a number of different clinical trials. What do you know about the different levels or 'phases' of clinical trials

   Clinical trials are carried out across a number of different 'phases', which relate to how mature the treatment being investigated is. Each phase has a different goal. For example, when considering a new drug therapy, Phase 0 trials tend to be very small and relate to determining the pharmacokinetics (such as bioavailability) of new treatment therapies. Phase 1 trials are designed to assess the safety of a new treatment, and so are carried out on small number of healthy volunteers to ensure there are no significant adverse reactions identified. Phase 2 trials are medium sized trials and aim to determine information more about the dose required for efficacy and the side effect profile of the treatment. Phase 3 trials are large trials that look to compare the new therapy against the existing standard treatment to see if there is any improvement in outcomes, as well as to look in further depth at the side-effect profile. Finally, Phase 4 trials relate to large studies being performed after the drug has been approved, and are designed to look at long-term efficacy as well as rarer side effects that may not have been obvious initially.

Example 3:

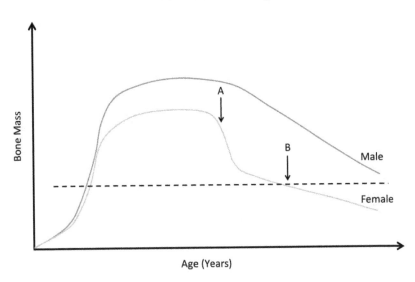

Bone Mass vs Age

Questions:

1. What does this graph show?

2. What is illustrated by the arrow A? Why might this be?

3. What might the dotted line shown by B indicate?

4. What may be the significance of the pink line dropping below the dotted line?

Answers:

1. What does this graph show?

    The graph shows the bone mass over time for both male and female populations. The graph shows an initial prominent and consistent rise for both populations, before the male population goes on to a higher overall bone mass. Both populations then show a decline in bone mass with age.

2. What is illustrated by the arrow A? Why might this be?

    The arrow A illustrates a sharp reduction in the bone density within the female population. The likely explanation for this is that this may be when the female population goes through menopause.

3. What might the dotted line shown by B indicate?

    The dotted line shown by B is a horizontal line that cuts through the graph and sits at a relatively low level of overall bone mass. This line may therefore represent a clinical definition of low bone mass (such as osteopaenia or osteoporosis).

4. What may be the significance of the pink line dropping below the dotted line?

    As mentioned, the significance of the line dropping below the dotted line might be that the population has entered an area of low bone mass. This may effectively show the population of patients suffering from osteoporosis: which, as the graph shows, is very common in elderly women. The patients within this population may require close monitoring with bone density imaging, or may indeed require treatment with calcium supplements or bisphosphonates.

Top Tip! Question 3 can be a tricky one: you may be faced with questions that ask seemingly arbitrary questions about aspects of the graph or data that you are unsure of. Again, the key is to take time to think, then logically talk your way through what is shown, and use that time to come up with an answer that is insightful and logical. The interviewers will be impressed!

PRESENTATIONS

Certain deaneries may ask you to prepare and give a presentation during your interview. The way this normally works is that they will provide you with one or more scientific papers, in advance of the interview, and ask you to prepare a presentation to give on the day. You will provide your PowerPoint slides prior to the interview day. The presentations themselves can be variable in their length: some deaneries have a 10 minute station where the presentation should last 5 minutes with 5 minutes for questioning, and others allow 20 minutes (10 minutes for the presentation itself, and 10 minutes for questioning). Generally, candidates are given at least two weeks to prepare their presentations in advance.

The topics that come up for presentation can vary. Frequently, the presentations ask you to critically appraise one or more research papers. A discussion of how to critically appraise a paper is beyond the scope of this book, but (as covered in the previous chapter) we do suggest that you focus some time on learning the hierarchy of medical evidence and how to properly appraise a scientific study. The authors would also suggest to candidates that it is important not to be too critical of any specific paper: if there are weaknesses then it is important that you point them out, but if you find yourself identifying a large number of minor points then it may be wise to choose to skip over some of them. You don't want to come across in an overly negative way to your interviewers.

General Presentation Advice

We are sure that at this stage in your medical student career you will be confident preparing and delivering presentations. However, it always helps to go over some of the key points.

1. Ensure you address the key requirements set out in the brief.

2. Related to this, ensure that you have practiced your presentation several times in the run up to the actual day so that you are completely confident with what you are presenting. This will also allow you to know that you will not overrun your time slot.

3. Pitch your interview at the right level – if you are presenting a scientific paper then remember that you are addressing medical professionals, but that they may not be experts in that particular field.

4. Practice answering questions, and prepare answers in advance for what you think the most common questions are likely to be.

5. Ensure you aim for the rule of roughly one slide per minute (depending on how dense with information that particular slide is, of course)

6. If you can do so delicately, then you can aim to slip in little details of your academic achievements if they are somehow related to the topic of presentation.

7. Spend equal time addressing all members of your audience – it is important that no interviewer feels left out when you are delivering your presentation.

8. As is the case with the interview itself, ensure you are dressed appropriately in smart attire.

We will now provide some examples of several 'good' and 'bad' presentation slides, to give you an idea of some of the common pitfalls to avoid when designing your presentation. The key principle to try to follow is that your presentation should come across as totally professional, and avoiding some of the following mistakes is a good way to try to ensure this.

Example 1: Be Careful with Formatting

The first example, and one of the most important pieces of advice when preparing your presentation, is a discussion of good and bad slide formatting. You need the slide to look professional and to be easy for the interviewers to read. Therefore, it is important to choose appropriate backgrounds and fonts.

Good example:

Randomised Controlled Trials

- Gold standard for evaluating new treatments

- Carried out over several different phases, starting from Phase 0 through to Phase 4

- Ideally, both clinicians and patients should be blinded to the treatment

---

This presentation uses a simple black font on a white background, allowing for plenty of contrast between words and background, making it straightforward and easy for the interviewers to read.

Bad Example:

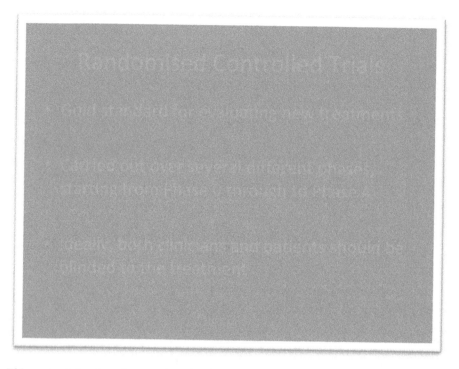

This presentation has chosen a blue background with pink font: clearly this is much more challenging to read and does not provide sufficient contrast to easily distinguish text from background. It can be tempting to try to make your presentation stand out from the crowd, but always try to do so in professional ways.

Another downfall seen when thinking about slide backgrounds is when presenters try to use images as a background. This rarely works and very often distracts from the content of the slide itself, so be extremely cautious if you are thinking of using an image as the background to your slides.

Bad Example:

> _**Randomised Controlled Trials**_
>
> - _Gold standard for evaluating new treatments_
>
> - _Carried out over several different phases, starting from Phase 0 through to Phase 4_
>
> - _Ideally, both clinicians and patients should be blinded to the treatment_

Here, the background and colour are fine, but the font itself is difficult to read. Font is another area to be careful with: it is safest and most professional to stick to one of the classically used and easy to read fonts such as Times New Roman, Arial or Calibri.

Example 2: Too Much Information

One of the most common mistakes when writing a presentation is to include too much information on each slide: we are sure you have experienced this plenty of times during medical school lectures! Just think about how difficult it was to follow the lecturer when you were trying to read large chunks of text on each slide. Or even worse, how dull it was if each slide was full of text and the lecturer was simply reading from the slides.

The slides should serve as prompts for you, and do not need to specifically show all the information that you are going to tell the interviewers as part of your presentation. This helps reduce the clutter on your slides, and also helps keep the listeners engaged, as they actually have to listen to you!

Good Example:

Osteoporosis

- A disease of low bone density

- Increased likelihood of fragility fractures

- Much more common in the elderly and in women

- Treatments include calcium supplements and bisphosphonates

This slide has the correct amount of information: each bullet point serves as a sort of sub-heading from which the presenter can expand on what they intend to tell the listeners.

Bad Example:

Osteoporosis

- A disease of low bone density (density is 2.5 standard deviations below the reference measurement).
- Increased likelihood of fragility fractures, which are defined as fractures that shouldn't have occurred with the level of force that caused them.
- Much more common in the elderly and in women, with the rates of incidence increasing significantly after the menopause.
- Treatments include calcium supplements such as Adcal and bisphosphonates such as alendronic acid.

The presenter has included too much information on this slide: it is difficult for the listeners to read all of it, and even if they do it probably means they are not listening to what you are saying.

Therefore, ensure that the slides you prepare are not serving as your script, and that they have short sub-headings that you will be able to expand on when you cover each point in more detail.

Example 3: Keep Images Large

Having images in your presentation is a useful way to break up the visual monotony of most presentations and to give your examiners something to look at when you are talking. A good image can convey more information than you could by speaking.

Good Example:

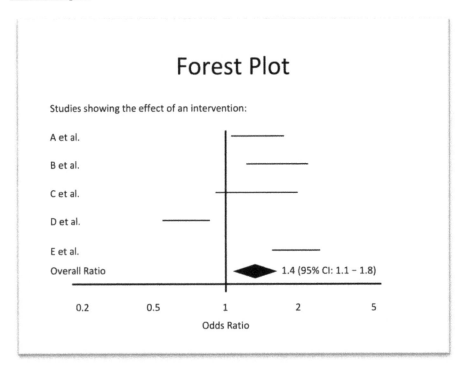

In this case, the image takes up the whole slide, and gives plenty of space for the listeners' gaze to move around the slide. It provides a good starting point for the presenter to go on to describe individual aspects of the image itself.

Bad Example:

Forest Plot

- **5 studies were included**

- **Overall Odds Ratio was 1.4**

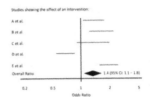

This image is clearly way too small. It is much harder to pick out the individual elements of the slide such as the findings of the different trials, and the confidence interval. The presenter has written some bullet points beside the slide to try to explain what is in the graph, but with a larger graph they would be able to do this verbally and so more engagingly for the audience.

Therefore, remember – if you have images in your presentation – ensure you present them large enough for all of the fine details to be easily read.

Example 4: Ensure Your Images Project Well

A fairly common phrase heard during presentations is 'This image shows xxxxx. I am sorry it is hard to see, it doesn't project well.' It may be true that certain images do project worse, but there are things you can do in advance to avoid this somewhat unprofessional situation.

Practise your presentation in advance – on a projector – so you can see if any of your images look poor when projected. This gives you time to either change the images completely, or to edit them to ensure they get your point across well. Settings to play with include the contrast, brightness and saturation of your images.

Good Example:

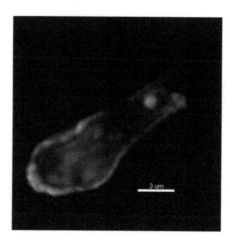

This image is clear, sufficiently bright and of a sufficient resolution for the audience to fully appreciate the points that the presenter is trying to make.

Bad Example:

This image is too washed out – too low in contrast and saturation – to ever 'project well', and needs work or changing before being used in a presentation.

Another aspect of your images to be wary of when preparing your presentation is their resolution. Be careful that you do not use any low resolution images as they look poor and can be hard to read: this is often obvious when presenters take logos for their hospital or research institute from the internet and copy them into their powerpoint files without realising that the resolution is extremely low. This gives a grainy result, which, again, is hard to read and looks unprofessional.

Images are critical components of good presentations, and it is your responsibility to ensure that they do indeed 'project well' prior to the presentation itself. It is important that your presentation comes across as completely professional to the interviewers, and ensuring there are no technical faults is one good way to do this.

Example 5: Be Sparing with Animations

This, of course, is a difficult topic to provide example slides of on a static book page. However, it is a straightforward topic to consider, and one to be careful of in your presentations.

Animations should only be used when they serve a purpose – for example, if they result in subsequent bullet points appearing after the prior point is discussed. This can be a useful way for presenters to focus the listeners' attention on a specific point, and to ensure that the topics are discussed in a set order.

However, it can be easy to go over the top with animations in an attempt to make your presentation stand out and appear exciting. Resist the temptation to have images 'fly' in across the slide. Also try to resist the temptation to have major transition animations when moving from one slide to the next: they are rarely, if ever, required.

Therefore, make sure you are very sparing with animations. Too many animations can lead to distraction, and may make the interviewers think you are attempting to hide a lack of meaningful content within your presentation. Using animations only when required shows good presentation technique, which is clearly something that the interviewers are looking to assess during this station.

FINAL ADVICE

You should now have a greater understanding of what to expect from the AFP application and interviews. We hope that you are now looking forward to the opportunity to show your potential interviewers the enthusiasm that you have for the prospect of combining a career in both medical research and clinical medicine.

Make sure you complete each and every section of the application to the best of your ability, and think about how what you write can be used to frame questions in the interview itself. Devote enough time to the preparation of your presentation, and make sure you practice it in front of an audience so you are completely confident that you will complete it in the time allotted!

It is important to ensure that you spend enough time preparing for the interview – practice interviews are the key! – such that you are no longer unsure of how you may respond on the day, and so you are familiar with responding to the type of questions you are most likely to be asked. Don't forget the likelihood that a clinical element will be present in the interview, and so try be up to date with the underlying medical knowledge required.

We hope that the guidance and information provided throughout this book will make you feel much more confident as the interview approaches, and most importantly will let your true enthusiasm shine through.

Good luck!

Dr Charles Earnshaw and Dr Rohan Agarwal

Acknowledgements

Charles Earnshaw is funded by a National Institute for Health Research Academic Clinical Fellowship.

WORK WITH UNIADMISSIONS

UniAdmissions is the UK's number one university admissions company, specialising in **supporting applications to Medical School and to Oxbridge**. Every year, *we* help thousands of applicants and schools across the UK. From free resources to these *Ultimate Guide Books* and from intensive courses to bespoke individual tuition, *UniAdmissions* boasts a team of **500 Expert Tutors** and a proven track record of producing great results.

UniAdmissions is always looking for enthusiastic tutors to help nurture tomorrow's talent. In addition to gaining valuable teaching and training skills, tutoring with us allows you to gain vital application points for your core medical or surgical training applications. All our medical tutors have the option of completing free teaching and training courses to help give their medical/surgical applications a much needed boost and stand out from the crowd.

To find out more visit: **www.uniadmissions.co.uk/work-with-us**

YOUR FREE BOOK

Thanks for purchasing this Ultimate Guide Book. Readers like you have the power to make or break a book – hopefully you found this one useful and informative. If you have time, we would love to hear about your experiences with this book.

As thanks for your time we'll send you another ebook from our Ultimate Guide series absolutely <u>FREE</u>!

How to Redeem Your Free Ebook in 3 Easy Steps

1) Find the book you have either on your Amazon purchase history or your email receipt to help find the book on Amazon.

2) On the product page at the Customer Reviews area, click on 'Write a customer review'

Write your review and post it! Copy the review page or take a screen shot of the review you have left.

4) Head over to www.uniadmissions.co.uk/free-book and select your chosen free ebook! You can choose from:
   ✓ The Ultimate OSCE History Guide
   ✓ The Ultimate FPAS SJT Guide
   ✓ The Ultimate IMT Application Guide
   ✓ The Ultimate CST Application Guide

Your ebook will then be emailed to you – it's as simple as that!

Alternatively, you can buy all the above titles at **www.uniadmisions.co.uk/our-books**

CPSIA information can be obtained
at www.ICGtesting.com
Printed in the USA
LVHW081304221119
638185LV00014B/453/P